Oxfam.
West-Wickham.
£ 1.49

Cue Frank!

To Nest. Joe Bough was right.

Cue Frank!

FRANK BOUGH

Queen Anne Press
Macdonald Futura Publishers
London

ACKNOWLEDGEMENT

Thank you to Penny Wood. Not the least of her considerable
talents is that she can read my writing.

First published in 1980 by Queen Anne Press,
Macdonald Futura Publishers Limited, Paulton House,
8 Shepherdess Walk, London N1 7LW

ISBN 0362 00519 2

Filmset by The Yale Press, London SE25

Printed and bound in Great Britain by Richard Clay (The
Chaucer Press) Limited, Bungay, Suffolk

CONTENTS

1

SCENE-SETTER

Like all upholsterers, Austin Joseph Bough spent a large part of his working life with a mouthful of tin tacks. A large part of his life *was* work, too, transforming innumerable broken-down three-piece suites into plump, comfortable seats for the blue bottoms of the burghers of Oswestry and district. I can see him now, feeding tacks from his mouth into his left hand, as he hammered away with his right.

But there was one time during the week, and one place, where you could always be sure of finding him – and that was on Saturday, in front of a television set watching BBC's *Grandstand*. At lunchtime in particular you would find him there, because that was when Fight of the Week was on, and of all the sports he loved boxing most of all. In the late fifties and early sixties, *Grandstand* carried all the best fights from all over the world, mostly American of course, and he never missed one. Whenever possible, Dad always insisted on having sausage and mash for lunch, because he reckoned it was the one meal you could always tuck into without taking your eyes from the screen.

I know this sounds a pretty pat and convenient way to launch into a few stories of fifteen years on the box, but it's absolutely true that he'd say to me sometimes: 'You know, *you* could do that job, you're interested in sport, you're always on a stage somewhere performing your socks off, given half a chance. It'd suit you down to the ground.'

Well, it's history now. For ten years or more I have done the very job he talked about, presenting the world's most adven-turous and innovative television sports programme, and a great many others besides. This year, 1980, *Grandstand* celebrates its twenty-second anniversary, and the only sad part of this story is that Dad never lived long enough to see his prediction come true. The fog of furniture dust that surrounded him all his life probably helped to feed the cancer that killed him in 1963, at the unreasonably early age of fifty-nine. I like to think, though, that when the champagne corks pop in celebration of *Grandstand*'s anniversary he'll be at the party in spirit, still feeding his face with sausage and mash, eyes firmly fixed on BBC-1, fed live by satellite to the heavenly kingdom he so richly deserved.

I must tell you some other time all the stories about Mum and Dad Bough – *'She's my Annie, I'm her Joe'*, he used to sing. Family life these days takes a hell of a buffeting but nobody has yet thought of a better way of living, and mercifully a great many youngsters still want to get married in the old-fashioned way, live together forever and produce kids. When you think about it, of course, most people get married when they are inexperienced, i.e. too young, and emotionally disturbed, i.e. in love. No businessman would ever make the most important decision of his professional life given those two propositions! But at least Mum and Dad got married to stay married, and when the hurdles came along, as they do in even the most ideal of relationships, they hauled each other over and pressed on. As for bringing up a family, who ever had any training for that either? Every day there are new decisions to be made, and we stumble from one compromise to the other.

That my sister, Mary, and I were happy was probably due to the fact that Mum and Dad were (is, in the case of Annie – happily, she's still with us!) two straightforward people, unencumbered with too many theories about life. Something else that suited us both very well was that Dad, out of work, had brought the family in 1939, when Mary and I were very young, from Stoke-on-Trent to Oswestry in Shropshire, a small market town bordered on three sides, within a mile or two, by Wales. (I was later ensnared by a Welsh girl who came marauding over the border as the Welsh have done in those parts for centuries, but we'll come to that presently.) It was a glorious place to be brought up in; a small community of some ten thousand souls, magnificent countryside all around, the Shropshire plain to the east and the Berwyn Mountains rising westwards out of the town in long folds up to Snowdonia and away to Cardigan Bay. What pleasure such a place had in store for a growing boy. Penylan, Croeswylan, Candy, there was a web of tiny lanes, all thick-hedged, winding out of the town. Catkins, primroses, hazelnuts, banks of blackberries, wild strawberries – all came in season to be plundered and enjoyed. There were deep woods with secret lakes, dark places where you could dream of conquering the world, streams that played music over their stones, and mountain peaks where you could see forever.

It was a natural playground. Nobody has ever devised a 'leisure centre' that can come anywhere near it. And later, what a place for the breathless fumblings of adolescence: the grassy banks are still there, reviving memories of Ruby, Rita, Wendy and Betty. (Did they *really* have names like that?)

Oswestry was where I learnt about music. With the Welsh everywhere, it was unavoidable. Blessed with a pure boy soprano voice, I started with *Where the Bee Sucks* at speech day on the stage of the drill hall, and then, encouraged by a marvellous teacher and choirmaster, Harry Moore-Bridger, graduated to the International Eisteddfod at Llangollen. All was sheer pleasure. And of course there was drama too – where else in a small town high school could I have played Hamlet, Shylock, Macbeth and Malvolio before I was nineteen?

Then there was always sport – any sport: school football, for instance, on a pitch up Penylan Lane with a slope on it as steep as Cader Idris. If you played centre-half, as I did, and stood on the penalty spot, your eyes were just about level with the halfway line; and how the clogging, rain-soaked turf dragged at those old leather boots. If you'd have told me then that I was to play some years later on the manicured grass of Wembley Stadium, I'd have said you were mad.

School football on Saturday morning was followed by club hockey in the afternoon. I made my debut for Oswestry Hockey Club at Rhyl, on the left wing of course, where all novices learn their trade – though I've never understood why, because it is the most difficult position on the whole field. And hell, when the team coach had safely negotiated the hazardous Horseshoe Pass down into Llangollen on the way home, I was too young to be allowed into the boozer at the bottom! 'Border Ales, the Wine of Wales' – I graduated to it eventually.

The greatest joy of all was summer cricket. One place we played was Knockin, a village where the square was immaculate, but that was all. Off the square there was rich, deep meadow grass. I remember many years later Sir Learie Constantine, that great West Indian cricketer, saying to me: 'In cricket, there's always plenty of room in the air, Frank.'

9

That described Knockin to a tee. If you didn't hit the ball in the air, it didn't go anywhere. It was the place where the two Turner brothers were king: ferocious bowlers both, and tremendous hitters. They owned the field as well. Not many visiting sides won at Knockin.

Another cricket location was the local asylum at Bicton, where the inmates circled the boundary. (I never liked fielding in the deep at Bicton.) We also had fierce local 'derbies' with the other school in the town – University School it was called. What a pleasure to hit my first 50 against that lot and on their pitch. I can remember the shot that did it to this day . . . sweet as a nut past square leg. Oh, and then there were visits to Trent Bridge for the Test match. Nottingham was hours away, so it meant the school party leaving at six in the morning. Was the weather going to hold? Would the pop last out? Would we get in? I remember vividly, standing worried in the queue round that long high brick wall, and the relief at last of gaining a place on the grass. I'd gaze at that handsome pavilion in the distance – no boys allowed there – and watch the giants emerge: Hutton, Compton, Evans, Simpson, Miller, Lindwall. They have all since welcomed me inside and talked about those days of pleasure, as we from Oswestry Boys' High School sat on the grass and admired their skills. Joe Bough, where are you now?

Well, in those days he encouraged me in all the things I have mentioned. Not with words, because he wasn't a man of language. But when he had a moment, he'd slip down to the Oswestry ground when I was playing cricket. Yet he rarely came in: I'd spot him standing in the road looking over the hedge. He always maintained that when he came in properly I never made any runs, so he stayed out of sight.

My mother played her part too. Our family was a kind of Anglo-Saxon kibbutz because Annie also put in a full day's slog in the little workshop behind the house, making curtains, cushions, loose covers. She'd hammer away at the treadle of a sewing machine, and yet lunch would always be ready for us. Never once during our school lives did Mary or I ever suffer the hazards of a post-war school dinner. What steadiness and calmness I now have when a television programme is falling about my ears (and they do from time to time you know, though we'd never let the cracks show) comes from Annie Bough. A lady of immense common sense, she is now a much loved Gran, forever on a diet so she says, though it makes little difference to her shape, which is about five feet square!

If it all sounds an idyllically happy upbringing, that's because it was. And, you know, there was no feeling that I should engage in all those various activities because they would stand me in good stead in the big world ahead. Drama, music, sport, cadets, scouts, were all followed with enthusiasm simply because they were the greatest fun. All my father and mother were determined about was that I certainly wasn't going to spend my life with a mouthful of tin tacks. Of that Joe was absolutely certain.

Yet it all paid off. Faced with an entrance examination to Merton College, Oxford – here again encouraged by a marvellous friend and teacher, Fred Dickenson, because Mum and Dad had no idea of the hows and wherefores of study or universities – I found that in the all-important interview after the paper, the examiners were well impressed with my all-round enthusiasm for life and obviously decided to let me into Merton to leaven the intellectual bread of the place. I was certainly no academic.

I had an extraordinary stroke of luck there, too, with the essay by which great store is set in entrance exams to Oxford, because it is supposed to reveal the quality of mind and imagination of the student. The choice of subject was either 'Orthodoxy' or 'Furniture'. The huge majority of hopefuls, knowing nothing about furniture, ploughed away philosophically into orthodoxy, social or religious. One or two may have had a personal interest in the history of furniture or been lucky enough to live in a grand house stuffed with Sheraton or Chippendale, but I bet nobody else wrote about frames and webbing and flock and springs and those tin tacks and the way I'd seen my father build up a chair from nothing to a tight, plump roundness. I'm also a great expert, having helped him many times to deliver the finished product, on how to get very large settees through very small doorways! My description must have come as a refreshing change to the examiners.

Most days of my life, someone somewhere asks me how I got into television. At various times of a school year there are always a batch of letters from youngsters saying: 'Dear Mr Bough, I have to decide on my O Level options in the next few weeks. What subjects should I sit so that I can become a television presenter?' That is very difficult advice to give, because although most television performers have a newspaper background, and that's still the best way to tackle the problem, there's no logic at all in the way I did it. But at Oxford the first piece of the jigsaw that was to decide my life was put into place.

When I got to Merton, where I was to spend three beautiful years, I put my name down to play college football, and eventually got to a trial game at Iffley Road, where the University XI played. In my first year there was an excellent team there. It was the time when amateur soccer was in its pomp. Pegasus, the combined Oxford and Cambridge XI, the brainchild of Tommy Thompson, now chairman of the Football Association, had recently won the Amateur Cup. The final at Wembley in those days filled the place. In my second year I won a regular place in the Oxford side at centre-half. The great prize of course was a university Blue, only awarded to those who played in one match, that against Cambridge at Wembley in early December. Our coach that year was a pro – Ron Greenwood, now greatly respected as a true gentleman, and manager of England's football team.

Football made for a joyful life: we played two matches a week, had the best coaching in the world, enjoyed great companionship, and fitness came out of our ears. Greenwood used to say: 'You'll never make pro footballers, but you're supposed to be intelligent so let's harness the skills you do have to their optimum effect.' It was a privilege to hear him talk, and who better to give us advice than the man who has continued that tradition of intelligent football in the academy that is West Ham FC, and is now doing the same for England.

But cruellest of cruel, I was injured in late November, and spent a frustrating University Match sitting on the sidelines at Wembley instead of playing on that beautiful turf.

So, with only one year left up at Oxford, it was all or nothing. We had a new coach, and thus I began a long friendship with Jimmy Hill, that extraordinary character who has since made such a contribution to the game in this country and is now, like Columbus, helping in the football colonisation of America.

Jimmy always reckoned that he was the best scrubbed pro footballer in the game at that time. It was 1954, and he was playing for Fulham, so he'd get up each morning, have a shower, go to Craven Cottage, train with Fulham, have another shower, leave for Oxford, where he'd lay into us (and I still remember the pain of his training routines, dashing from touch line to touch line until our thighs trembled and our lungs were stretched fit to burst). After another shower, it was back to London where he then had another job training a London amateur club – and of course another shower. It all kept him clean and trim he'd say. And by the way, Jimmy in those days was paid twenty pounds by Fulham, his Oxford coaching session brought in another two pounds ten, and his London coaching paid another couple of pounds. No wonder he successfully campaigned for the abolition of the maximum wage, for which today's wealthy young footballers should be truly grateful.

Although I was Oxford's regular centre-half that term, nothing is ever certain, so it was with great delight that I received the personal note from Harry Joynt, the 1954 captain, inviting me to represent Oxford University in the annual fixture against Cambridge. I'd got my Blue, as long as I could keep myself in one piece in the week or two before the match. I hardly dared to go out for fear of having some accident or other, but I made it. The whole family came to Wembley to see the game. I wish I could report a happy ending to my university football career, but it was not to be. Oxford went two up by half-time, with a strong wind at our backs, but we lost in the end by three goals to two. To say the least I hardly distinguished myself, particularly since the Cambridge centre-forward, called Brough, oddly enough, got a hat-trick. And I was a stopper centre-half to boot!

But nothing in sport will ever be as deeply satisfying as were those days of university football. It was played as hard as hell, but scrupulously fairly. That lovely man Danny Blanchflower recently described my sentiments perfectly: 'What football is about is going through something, going through it with others and emerging and feeling a sense of comradeship, of unity. You reach out and give something to the others and take something back from them and there's a bond of trust and respect. That's the real thrill and beauty of the game. Winning is terrific but it doesn't compare with that.'

The Irishman's words are a condemnation of the meanness of spirit that so often pervades football today, with so many players behaving like adolescents – petulantly throwing the ball away when a throw-in is given against them, and badgering the referee at virtually every decision in the hope that they'll wear him down to such an extent that eventually he'll give in. Mercifully, referees rarely do, which makes the players' behaviour even more stupid. The professional foul, too, is a cynical device cold-bloodedly intended to deny the opposition the fruits of their skill and imagination.

The game of football doesn't belong to any one player, or . any one club, to abuse in that manner. Unless it is protected from such treatment, and there are many in the professional game with the character and influence to do so, we'll lose one of the loveliest of all sports. Ominously the cancer spreads. Go to any local youth league and you'll see some of the young-sters, tomorrow's players, arguing vehemently with referees, while demented parents and team managers compound the aggravation from the touch line. 'You reach out and give something to the others and take something back from them, and there's a bond of trust and unity. Winning is terrific but it doesn't compare with that.' Good luck, Danny.

That Oxford Blue, for which I'd trained and sweated, for no other reason than that it gave me the most tremendous fun and satisfaction, was to prove really decisive in the career I was ultimately to follow. To start with, it was to take me to the north-east of England, because in my last term at Merton, David Swarbrick, an Old Mertonian, and a former England rugby international, asked me if I'd ever thought of joining ICI for my first job. They had a huge factory at Billingham-on-Tees (it's nine miles around the fence – I know, I've walked every inch of it) and they had a football team in the Northern League called Billingham Synthonia (Synthetic Ammonia – got it?) Recreation. The Northern League in those days, the fifties, was one of the amateur game's great strongholds, and there was fearsome competition between clubs like Crook Town and Bishop Auckland, as well as the clubs in the Southern Amateur League, like Walthamstow and Hendon. Some great characters appeared, too; like Bob Hardisty of Bishop Auckland, who became a legendary figure in the amateur game, and goalkeeper Harry Stanatt – Flash Harry, they called him, but a fine keeper. I think Lionel Wharton, the labour department manager at ICI Billingham, only really wanted me to play football for Synthonia, but I went to see him nevertheless. Two years later I joined ICI to practise O & M – Organisation and Methods. I was going to be a captain of industry.

I say two years, because after university I still had National Service to do and again something happened which in the end decided I was never to become chairman of ICI. I served queen and country in the Royal Tank Regiment, and that shouldn't have happened either, because a mile outside Oswestry was Park Hall camp from which generations of gunners have been welded into shape by the drill sergeants of 64 and 68 Royal Artillery Regiments. I say welded because I still meet many men who ask me where I come from. 'Oswestry? My God', remembering the scars of those sixteen terrifying weeks of basic training, 'do people actually live there?'

I applied to join the Gunners. I could see myself getting home for lunch. So too could the Selection Board; so I was sent to Carlisle to the Royal Armoured Corps. On the train I regularly met a native of Carlisle who was stationed in Oswestry. We both agreed we could have saved the army a great deal in travelling expenses if we'd both stayed at home.

So off I went to Germany, as a fresh-faced 2nd Lieutenant, to Munster, to join the 2nd Royal Tank Regiment. A real education, the army. They put me in charge of four large Centurion tanks, and on one terrifying journey from the training area outside Munster back to barracks, I somehow lost the designated route, the surface of which had been reinforced specifically to cope with the heavy tracks. What a nightmare that was, manoeuvring four huge tanks in the narrow backstreets of downtown Munster. It was customary when travelling to clamp the main gun back over the engine decks, and during one rather complicated manoeuvre round a rather sharp corner I turned round in my turret to see the end of the barrel nudging a neat hole in the wall of some poor burgher's house. We fled!

While in Germany I met Chris Bonnington, who is now one of the world's finest mountaineers, with an Everest conquest to his considerable credit. The army had succeeded in stationing Chris on the flattest part of the North German Plain. He spent most of his leisure time driving miles to find some kind of rock face on which to practise his craft. I hope Chris won't mind too much if I recall in the same breath another memorable encounter, with a lady in Hamburg, whose *pièce de resistance,* if one can call it that, was to place six matches in her pubic hair, set them alight and say 'Iss goot, *ja?* Iss Christmas tree!'. Happily she blew the candles out before the whole forest went up in flames.

One day I had a call from Gerald Sinstadt. Viewers in ITV's Granada-land will know him now as a first-rate football commentator, but at that time he was the sports editor of the

British Forces radio broadcasting network, based in Cologne. He did just about everything, including the station football commentaries, for which he used one or two army personnel to help out. It seemed that his summariser had been posted to the Hook of Holland, which put him right out of court. He'd stuck a pin on to a list of football-playing soldiers, my name was on the end of it, and would I like to try my hand at helping him out. Well, I only did two jobs for him – an Army Cup game between two regiments, and West Germany versus Scotland. A fair spread, I thought! Years later I was to be extremely grateful to Gerry Sinstadt's pin, and to some very thoughtful advice he gave me when it mattered most. Much as I'd enjoyed the thrill of handling my first microphone, I wasn't to realise at the time that it was the beginning of an immensely fascinating, frustrating but rewarding way of life.

National Service was the greatest contraceptive ever invented. Nobody could afford to support a family on the pay, so there was no opportunity, thank heavens, of rushing into hasty marriages. Many a young man escaped disaster by the skin of his teeth, simply because he couldn't leap straight into matrimony when he felt like it. When the first flush of romance had worn off, and he realised that the lady was not the girl of his dreams, he breathed a sigh of relief, and moved a heartfelt vote of thanks to the Ministry of Defence for keeping him out of trouble.

However, I did make my reservation, as it were, while I was in Munster. In my later years at college, and particularly during the early part of my National Service, I found myself more and more in the company of a Welsh girl called Nest Howells. Come to think of it, the place we met, the Garrison Theatre at Park Hall Camp, Oswestry, is not the most auspicious start to a lifetime of marital bliss. It was a dance hall where a thousand heavy-booted squaddies sought refuge from their tormentors, in the hope of a bit of kiss and cuddle at least from the local totties, and in particular the nurses from the local orthopaedic hospital, where there was a training school. Between the camp and the hospital was a mile-long, wooded lane, known as the Burma road, and it took a strong-minded girl to survive the sexual gunfire that thundered the length of it after the Saturday night hop, when passions were inflamed by the strict tempo of George Riley and his band. Remember the Beatles hadn't been invented in 1956, Radio I was inconceivable, and the hottest sound around was Joe Loss.

Nest was training to become a physiotherapist, we saw more of each other, and I suppose it was my father who put the seal on the whole thing. He had always been extremely critical of my girlfriends. I know what he went through now. Parents, however much they say they don't influence their offspring's relationships, do like to like the friends they like! Dad adored Nest, and one day, slightly embarrassed, because ours was not a household where we talked easily about relationships, he said: 'You'll never do better than that, my son.'

I came to much the same conclusion, so in November 1956, when the 2nd Royal Tank Regiment had its annual thrash to celebrate the battle of Cambrai, I had my battle plans ready. Cambrai was the occasion in World War I when tanks were used in combat for the first time, and it was an anniversary celebrated in the regiment with unparalleled bacchanalia.

The bachelors amongst us organised a plane to fly over from Southend packed with beauties to celebrate with us, and I asked Nest to come. It was a memorable weekend. Mind you, deciding to ask somebody to marry you is all very well, when the rockets are going off, and the heart is leaping with joy, but my God, it's frightening as well. Imagine the scenario with me. I asked Nest when the all-night Celebration Ball was at its height. It was 5am, the time when traditionally the enemy attacks because the opposition's morale is at its lowest. I still wonder to this day who was the aggressor on that occasion, because at 7am, two hours later, Nest was on a plane back to England; and at eight I was on parade, slightly hungover, and wondering whether it was all a dream, or if it wasn't, what the hell had I gone and done!

Word had got around the barracks that Bough had popped the question at five in the morning. 'You're mad', said the adjutant, Dicky Everard, a confirmed bachelor. 'If it's to be done at all, and that's extremely doubtful, it should be done stone-cold sober and in the clear light of day.'

It turned out he was wrong. Twenty-one years later we are still good friends, and more in love than ever before. I differentiate because they are two entirely different, though essential, ingredients for an exciting marriage. It could also have something to do with the fact that Nest is Welsh. In Wales they are proud to say of their women that they are 'pious in chapel, shrewd in the market-place, and frantic in

17

bed'. Apart from the fact that sometimes Nest doesn't shop too well, I've never complained!

So in 1958, fresh out of the army, with a wife-to-be in one hand and a job in the other, I set off to make my fortune at Imperial Chemical Industries. That I was starting at rock bottom there was no doubt. We hadn't a penny. In fact, there was no way we could get married immediately because Nest hadn't finished her training and although qualified physio-therapists in the National Health service earned a paltry salary, and still do, her few pounds were going to be essential to the family budget. So she stayed to finish her course at Oswestry and I went to scout out the land that was to be our first home, the north-east of England.

I took digs with Vi and Ernie Watson in Addison Road, Middlesbrough. Ernie had 'the bronchitis' as Vi called it. Movement of any kind was an effort. In fact Ernie had long since stopped going upstairs and slept in the living room. He occasionally stepped out and I remember we once went together to Ayresome Park, where Middlesbrough played football. It was at the end of the road, all of fifty yards away, where a young footballer called Brian Clough was the idol of the fans, scoring thirty goals or so, regularly every season, and already showed signs of becoming an ebullient leader of men off the field. His shop-steward tactics on behalf of the team against poor Bob Dennison, the manager, gave the *Middlesbrough Gazette* plenty of copy.

Ernie's problem was the winter, which on Teesside can be hard, to say the least. Each one was a steeplechase, with life or death as the prize. He'd cough and wheeze his way triumphantly into the spring and spend the summer building up what resistance he had to his bronchitis ready for the off again in November. Finally he fell; remembered as a gentle, considerate man, and a master with the Yorkshire pudding. Only *he* made them on Sunday, nobody else, and they were served Yorkshire fashion, by themselves, before the beef but covered in its gravy. They were unbeatable.

Ernie was one of those people who encouraged me in the belief that millionaires on their death beds don't think too much of the villa in Spain, the yacht in Cannes harbour or the Rolls in the garage, but of the friends they've made in life. Relationships are most elusive. On the one hand are those folk with whom you know you'll never have any sympathy, since their behaviour and the way they treat people is so abhorrent that there's no common ground at all, and on the other, the friendships that give a pleasure that is far beyond the enjoyment of material possessions. I'm sure you know what I mean.

Such a friend was Eddie Cairney, whom I first met when I went to Billingham ICI. He is a delightful Scot, with a great sense of humour, and a gentleness of manner that shows itself particularly when he is in his cups. Unlike most Scots, who want to beat the living daylights out of you when they've had a few, Eddie slides happily down the wall, serenity in his face, intoning a terrible dirge called *Mackintosh's Lament.* Will somebody explain to me why all the Scots in England are so full of sparkling wit, while those who stay north of the border always seem steady, if not dour?

When Nest joined me in Middlesbrough, newly qualified as a physiotherapist, she and I, plus Eddie and his fiancée, Pat, all went to live together in Stokesley. Well, not really, because that kind of thing didn't go on in 1958. The girls had a cottage on the Green, and Eddie and I actually shared a double bed across the alleyway in digs with Mr and Mrs Gent. The curious thing is that these days, nobody would turn a hair had we set up with the girls, and bedded them as a kind of trial run for matrimony: what people find odd now is that Eddie and I shared the double bed! Life does take funny twists and turns. We are all still happily married, so neither our choice, nor our early sleeping habits, let us down!

However, I was finding that ICI wasn't really me. For some, I'm sure the study of Organisation and Methods is a fantastic subject: designing, for example, a smooth system for administering the distribution of sulphuric acid or nitrochalk fertiliser and the forms to go with it. I don't think I had it! I found I was pouring far more of my energy into my leisure time with the Middlesbrough Little Theatre – yes, I was back on the stage again, for the first time since school – than into my working day. I had a right dust-up one Tuesday afternoon with the boss, who discovered I had sneaked away to watch the university rugby match on the telly. I was beginning to cheat, and to look forward to five-thirty, and that's no way to spend a life. I thought back to Germany, the army, Gerald Sinstadt and those two radio contributions I'd made to the forces network. I started writing letters to the BBC, telling them I was God's gift to the broadcasting industry, and if they didn't employ me immediately in some capacity or other, they'd go bust. Come to think of it, they've almost done that since I've joined them!

Somehow the Beeb didn't quite see it that way; obviously they were convinced that they could survive without me, and I've still got the pile of polite refusals telling me so. Only once, and I'm talking of eighteen months badgering on my part, did I ever get a hearing. I answered an advert for a BBC announcer's job, and was actually asked to report to a BBC establishment in London. Great excitement ... train to King's Cross, tube to Broadcasting House. The only person I met was the commissionaire on the door, who took my name, and led me through a maze of corridors to a room that resembled a large padded cell. It was absolutely empty save for a lectern standing in the middle of the floor. Just like Big Brother, a voice boomed at me, from out of the wall some-where. 'Good morning, Mr Bruff.' (My name can be a terrible problem. The permutations of pronunciation are endless. Think of cough, though, through, bough, thorough, say them aloud and you'll see what I mean – only last week I heard a woman say to her mate, 'Look, there's Peter Brough'!). 'Good morning, Mr Bruff – you'll find on the lectern several scripted announcements. Will you read them for us one by one.' On one was a news bulletin, on another a weather forecast, on a third the programme for an orchestral concert with Saint Saëns, Khachaturian, Mahler – I did my best. The wall said 'Thank you, Mr Bruff', the commissionaire came in and led me back to the front door, and in five minutes flat I was back on the pavement in Portland Place!

A week later another letter went on to the pile. 'Thank you for your attendance at the audition but we're afraid etc etc.' I designed a few more forms, worked out an efficient system of delivering the post to innumerable sheds, offices and plants in the huge ICI factory at Billingham and started again.

This time I cracked it. I switched on the television one night and there, wonder of wonders, was Gerald Sinstadt, giving a sports news round-up. He'd obviously left army broadcasting and got a job with the BBC. I wrote him a letter. By this time I was a past master, but to Gerry it was different. I didn't ask him to help me find a job, but simply to tell me how best to attack the BBC edifice. Where was it weakest, what was the best method of attack, where did the Corporation advertise that I didn't know about?

Now Gerry Sinstadt could have done one of two things: he

could have penned me a jolly little note saying nice to hear from you again, how are things going, yes it is tricky getting into the Beeb isn't it, you'll just have to keep whacking away, goodbye! But he didn't. He sat down, took great trouble over his reply, and laid out for me in a long letter all kinds of good advice. If you want to put your finger on it, it's because of his thoughtfulness that what's happened has happened, and that I'm telling you this story at all.

But the sentence that clinched it was 'Go and see Arthur Appleton in Newcastle'. Now, if you've never met Arthur Appleton, there are no words I know that can describe what a nugget he is. By all those who have met him, he is much loved as one of the world's great human beings. He's a Geordie, football daft, and his book on north-east football called *Hotbed of Soccer* is the most loving appreciation of that corner of the game I have ever read.

Arthur was a BBC radio producer at the BBC's New Bridge Street studios in Newcastle, responsible amongst other things for the *Sports Spotlight* radio programme which every Saturday evening fed the sport-hungry population of Tyne, Tees, and Wear with their Saturday diet of sports news and results. The contributors were made up of professionals like Harold Williamson, who has since made some of the very best television programmes with the *Man Alive* team on BBC-2. His 'children talking' programmes were masterly examples of the interviewer's craft, drawing wonderful responses from youngsters with gentle, thoughtful promptings. Another contributor was George House, one of the real professionals of regional broadcasting, radio and television, plus a ragbag collection of out of work actors, impecunious vicars, and moonlighting schoolteachers, all hell-bent on earning a fiver for a contribution to the programme, and at the same time enjoying a big ego trip.

'What do you really want to do?' asked Arthur, in that soft, Geordie voice. Here's a man, I thought, who'll cut through bullshit like butter. 'I just want to be a broadcaster', I said, 'very much. I think I can do it, but nobody will let me find out.' I was in luck. 'I do need a couple more part-time reporters', he said, 'and there are half a dozen likely blokes, plus a recording van going to the Darlington/Southport game to see what they can make of it. Come and join us.'

I tell you, that audition was a nightmare. Apart from all the anxiety in my soul, because here at last I had a chance and was desperately anxious for it not to go begging, there was another small complication. When we got to the match, threequarters of the Darlington ground was in thick fog. There was no place from which you could see more than twenty yards in any direction. The six of us split the match between us, and when the play went out of sight the commentary was sheer fiction!

The day was a disaster, and I resigned myself to form design for evermore. But dear Arthur had seen something, God knows what, and rang me to say that since the weather at Darlington had made the test pretty inconclusive, would I go to another match, travel back to the Newcastle studio afterwards, and record a minute's report on it.

Strangely enough, my biggest worry this time was that I had no motor car. ICI salaries at the time didn't rise to one, but John Gardner, a colleague, came to my aid. 'It's not much', he said, 'and it'll probably break down, but it's all I've got – take it'. How I have been blessed with good friends.

What an unlikely start to a career, travelling to Bishop Auckland for an amateur cup tie, in the depths of a north-east winter, with ice and snow everywhere, in an old Ford van! All I remember of that bitter day on the heights of County Durham was that the match was played, every high ball came down with snow on it and the Ford van kept going, and I loved it. I wrote a piece I was convinced warranted a Pulitzer prize at the very least, and delivered it into a microphone, five long years after my last effort for the 8th Hussars.

I sat with Arthur as the recording was played back. 'This is the moment', I thought, 'it all hangs on this one minute of voice'. Suddenly the report seemed banal, monotonous, totally without life. Arthur switched off the machine. He stoked his pipe, lit up again. 'What are you doing next Saturday afternoon?' he asked.

* * * * *

I've met so many people who recall that at eighteen they thought they had life in the palm of their hand, only to discover that all kinds of influence bear down to decide what they eventually do. It's all rather like the slices of a cake. One slice is your own aspirations, another your endeavour and hard work, another whatever particular skills or talent you happen to have. After that though, there are too many other slices over which you have no control whatsoever. A slice of luck, whom you meet, where you happen to be; while a very considerable slice is somebody else's decision. You'll recognise already several of those ingredients in my particular cake. Now to be added was the final slice that made the cake complete.

In the smaller regional centres of the BBC in 1962, which is where we now are, television was very small scale indeed. At Newcastle there was a tiny studio, only two cameras, if that, one telecine machine for playing film, and normally the only time that the region spoke to its own was in a short conventional news bulletin, lasting for perhaps five minutes at lunchtime and another five minutes in the evening before the main network news bulletin. This was certainly true of places like Plymouth, Southampton, Norwich and Newcastle, while the regional centres like Manchester, Birmingham and Bristol did little better, spending a lot of their time contributing material to other programmes, like news bulletins, current affairs and sport.

However, in 1962 the decision was taken to expand the role of the smaller station, to give it more air time, to allow it to reflect on the issues of the day in that area, to highlight the aspirations of the people, their character and sense of humour. The proposal was that each of the regions should be given twenty minutes early in the evening to make their own programmes for their own people. Even to this day it's the most significant change that has ever taken place in the history of BBC regional and national television, because Scotland and Wales and Northern Ireland, although they had already achieved a certain degree of national identity, were included as well.

In the spring, at the end of the football season, Arthur Appleton threw a small beer party, the best kind of party in the north-east. The beer is the best in Britain. It is also the only place I know where if you order a large Scotch you're presented with a pint of cold ale, because that's what it is called.

Arthur wanted to thank all those vicars, schoolteachers and associated part-time bric-a-brac (I was the only industrial representative as far as I was aware!) for their efforts on Saturdays on behalf of *Sports Spotlight*. At the shindig I was introduced to John Tisdall, who was at that time the BBC's north-east area news editor.

'Come and see my television camera', he said, and led me

across the road into the main BBC building, which, incidentally, had once been a lying-in hospital. Let's put it this way: it was hardly MGM, or Warner Brothers: two prototype electronic cameras in a tiny studio, basic lighting, a caption stand, and alongside it all a cramped control room no bigger than a corridor. We sat and talked, and he explained how the following autumn he had the job of launching a new twenty-minute evening news magazine programme from this very place. Ever so tentatively, he wondered if I would be at all interested in being considered as a possible member of the team he was putting together. He'd heard my radio pieces, he said (I'd only done three reports at the time), and would quite like to see how I performed in front of a camera.

So a series of tests were arranged, and in the summer I paid several visits to the television studio in Newcastle, to do a number of things: a straight piece to camera, in other words talking right into the lens; an interview, being interviewed. After a week John was sufficiently reassured to suggest that I should actually read one of the transmitted news bulletins, a standard conventional five-minuter, with captions and films. In June 1962 I went on to the television airwaves for the first time, and then again, the following night.

There is a pub alongside Broadcasting House in New Bridge Street called The Portland. You'd never call it a place of great beauty, but it is full of good beer, and brimming with Geordie character and individuality. On the Thursday of the second week of the auditions, John sat me down, and as I recollect, satisfied his own conscience by pointing out every objection he could think of to my becoming a broadcaster. 'Look', he said, 'what on earth do you want a job like this for? We've done a few tests, OK, and you're not bad, but there's a great divide between a close circuit audition in a cosy studio and actually going on air and stringing things together successfully one after the other. You could be a disaster. You've got a secure job with ICI, a pension fund, profit-sharing – you've got the responsibilities of a family.' (By this time there were two baby sons, David and Stephen.) 'And you know', he continued, 'this programme we're talking about is only scheduled for three months. It's very much on trial, and could be axed by Christmas, and then where would you be? I'll let you know.'

I left not knowing what he was going to do. When I got home I told Nest of the conversation and said I could think of six good reasons why I thought I'd get the job, and another six reasons which suggested I hadn't got a cat in hell's chance of being offered it.

On Saturday, John Tisdall rang. 'I'd like you to present *North At Six* for me', he said. 'That's what we're calling it. We open up in September.' I thanked him, put down the phone, and as I looked at Nest it must have shown. 'You'll want to do it properly', she said. 'Let's move up to Newcastle.'

Joe Bough was right. I couldn't have married better.

2
APPRENTICESHIP

She was called Alderman Mrs Theresa Russell, she was the mayor of Newcastle-upon-Tyne, she was my first ever television interviewee, and I forgot her name! What a start to my first programme. It wasn't that she'd come in to talk about civics, or politics, or the city's social problems. Theresa Russell was nuts about hats, and when she wasn't devoting her life to the citizenry of Tyneside, she was collecting hats, in any spare moment she had. She wore them all the time. I'm sure she had a special one for bed. In those early days of *North At Six*, or *Look North* as it came to be called (the name had to change, because the start time did – and no longer did we open up precisely at six), when we were weary of the region's high unemployment figures, or T. Dan Smith had gone quiet, which wasn't very often, or when Lord Hailsham in cloth cap and boots had gone away, we would ask Theresa Russell to bring in a few of her new hats to lighten our lives.

Forgetting her name was the start of a television apprenticeship which I was fortunate to be able to enjoy in Newcastle, because a BBC region is an excellent place to learn the broadcasting trade. That apprenticeship has been going on ever since. I'll tell you what I mean by that. You would have thought, wouldn't you, that having forgotten the name of my first interviewee, I'd have made damn certain that it didn't happen again. Well, you're right, and I devised several ways of having a new name, or a fact, hidden somewhere about my person in case my conversation wavered and I forgot it. A piece of paper on the desk in front of you is the obvious place, but that's not always possible, so the palm of the hand, up the shirt sleeve, even the inside jacket pocket – there are many ways. My system worked splendidly for years, and sure in the knowledge that should all else fail, my *aide memoire* was always at hand, I confidently identified footballers, prime ministers, film stars and the dozens of 'Mr and Mrs Canniebodies' from all over Britain I've interviewed since. But you know as well as I do that just when you think you know it all, life gets up and kicks you straight in the teeth. And so it was for names. I thought I'd got the problem whacked.

So I had, until one dreadful day at Fenner's Cricket Ground, Cambridge, several years after the Theresa Russell incident. It was the early days of Sunday cricket on BBC-2, that marvellous pioneering series of Sunday matches which went on for three years featuring the International Cavaliers. At a time when cricket was in the doldrums, and the three-day game was dying on its feet, the Cavaliers brought crowds, and a lot of fun back to the game. The example they set has spawned the Sunday League, and the other single day limited-overs competitions that have followed on.

The Cavaliers always started each series in early May, with a match at Fenner's against Oxford and Cambridge, past and present. The winning team won a cheque for £100 which was presented to the victorious skipper at the end of the match, preferably by some famous national personality.

Well, the man who was to do duty for us at Fenner's that day was very posh indeed. RAB Butler was a great politician who had held all the major offices of state bar one, that of prime minister. He thought he was going to get that too, but Harold Macmillan pipped him to it: always the bridegroom, never the bride. Nevertheless, a great famous Conservative politician, was Lord Butler; and he'd retired to the academic world to be Master of Trinity College, Cambridge. On each of the three occasions he made the presentation for us, I would reintroduce myself to him and explain the mechanics of the presentation: how a rope would be put out in front of the pavilion, near our low camera, to keep the crowds back; how I'd be in the middle of the group, with him on one side and the winning captain on the other. I'd introduce him, he'd hand over the cheque, say a few words if he liked, and then please stand back while I trailed next week's televised fixture and got off the air with dignity.

This worked splendidly for the first two years, and then on the third occasion I set up the tableau again while Jim Laker and John Arlott analysed the batting and bowling performances of the day. The winning captain joined us, and I indicated to Alan Mouncer, the producer, through the camera, that I was ready.

Alan cut to me on the low camera, and I started to make the

introduction. 'Well', I said, 'we've had a wonderful start to this season's Sunday cricket series. As you've seen, in a marvellously entertaining game' (like John Lewis, I never knowingly undersell!) 'the International Cavaliers have beaten Oxford and Cambridge past and present by 35 runs, and here's Ted Dexter, captain of the Cavaliers, to receive the winner's cheque presented by . . . ' I turned to his lordship, looked him straight in the eyes, and a great shutter came down over my stupid mind. There he stood, with that familiar crumpled face, part of the political fabric of the nation, and for the life of me I couldn't remember his name!

People often ask what happens if you dry up on television. Well, nearly all the television I do is live, so you can't dry up. You can't, in the middle of a programme, say 'Sorry folks, I've forgotten' and go home! You've got to say something and you'd be surprised what drives you on. You think of the wife and the kids, and the mortgage, and you keep going . . . So there I am, facing RAB Butler, mouth wide open, not knowing who he was. (And while you're laughing at my expense, how many times have you, at a party, turned to introduce an old friend, and just for a moment lost his name?)

So the next words to come out of my mouth, and I was fighting for my professional life by this time, were '. . . by my friend on my right'. After the whole sordid mess was over, Alan Mouncer consoled me, 'Well, Frank, I'll give you something', he said, 'at least you got his bloody politics right!'

Since Newcastle I've inherited some pretty famous programmes. I followed Peter Dimmock on to *Sportsview,* David Coleman into *Grandstand* and then Michael Barrett into *Nationwide,* but none of them has held quite the excitement of those early *Look North* days in Newcastle, in the autumn of 1962. Principally that's because we were creating something completely new, and I was doing what I really wanted to do for the very first time.

For a television programme, the budgets and the facilities were ludicrous. There were only those two cameras, which meant that if Harry Green, the director, wanted to point both of them at the same interview, which obviously he did, you had to be careful not to close the interview until out of the corner of your eye you'd seen one of the cameras trundling away across the studio to where it was needed next. Film was transmitted by way of one telecine machine, and if the film broke, which with hastily shot and processed newsfilm, was always possible, you had to keep talking about anything and everything, while they unstrapped it, rethreaded it and then gave you a wave to say you could lead back to it.

I wrote scripts, changed captions, welcomed the guests, briefed the interviewees, and poured the drinks afterwards. The team around me was fantastic, a luxury I've enjoyed ever since. That is the BBC's great strength – its depth of talent and the enthusiasm of its staff. It's something that the viewer is never aware of, but which helps make the BBC the finest broadcasting system in the world. John Tisdall led the programme team, Michael Alder was his senior assistant and their considerable talents have since been rewarded with high office elsewhere in the Corporation. George House, who as the experienced reporter had every reason to be disappointed that he hadn't been offered the main presenter's job, was a constant help. He knew the north-east like the back of his hand and would shoot off to report on film stories which ranged from the Seaham Harbour lifeboat disaster to the latest medical achievement at Newcastle Royal Infirmary. The delightful Tom Kilgour looked after and read the straight news bulletins we included in the programme. Harold Williamson was a regular contributor with beautifully observed contributions about the life and character of the region. He was the very best kind of regional commentator. He was fascinated by the north-east, and it took the network in London many years of careful seduction before he was persuaded to practise his talents before a wider audience.

The energy we all generated was tremendous, and although Nest and the family had moved up to Newcastle with me, they hardly saw me. There was only a small team, and we all needed to give 110 per cent to keep going. Five days a week we flogged away trying new ideas, keeping some, discarding others. We wanted the programme to have some visual identity, so some bright spark had the idea of an old-fashioned Victorian hatstand. Placed on the set for the opening shot, the plot was that the hats on the hooks suggested who was in the programme. 'You know', he said, 'if there's an admiral, a miner and a policeman on the programme, we'll hang their hats up for all to see'. That was all very well in theory, but far too often we had people on the programme who didn't wear hats at all!

For a while, I would walk in and hang my own hat on the hatstand as though I'd walked in off the street. (I had to buy one specially, because I never was a hat man.) In the end, we just left the thing standing there, unadorned, but it is extraordinary how many people still recall the programme and mention the old hatstand. It became its trademark.

After each programme, we'd get rid of the guests and pour into the Portland to toast the occasional success, and bemoan our inadequacies in the rich brown ale that is the local Geordie wine.

All the time I was trying to take stock of my own progress. Remember, the programme was scheduled for a three-month trial, and was to be reviewed at Christmas. The first chilling experience I had was to see my opposite number in Manchester, where they had then one programme for the north-west, finish after a fortnight. The presenter there was a young Lancashire-born actor and former schoolmaster called Colin Welland. He had made a great hit at Manchester's Library Theatre, being much applauded for his performances in Pinter's *The Birthday Party* and Behan's *The Hostage*, and was trying his hand at television. I suspect Colin's very individual maverick personality was too strong a meat for the conservative taste of BBC viewers at that time, and that, plus his preference for black open-necked shirts, didn't win him too many admirers. Over the Pennines in Newcastle, I swallowed hard when I heard he'd departed. Happily Colin's talents lay in other directions and since gaining fame in *Z Cars* he's become an actor/playwright of considerable stature.

However, *Look North* survived its trial period and I moved with it into a New Year, 1963, with another three-month contract. The BBC doesn't rush its fences! But several things began to happen to reassure me. The producer of a network sports programme called *Sportsview* (I was, by the way, still doing Radio Sport for Arthur Appleton on Saturdays) asked me to go to Huddersfield and do a film story on Anita Lonsborough, Britain's finest swimmer of the time. Another producer in Manchester, John Ammonds, had me over to that ancient chapel (at that time BBC Manchester's main studio, in Dickenson Road) to compère a programme called *Barn Dance,* all straw bales and check shirts and The Spinners. There were a lot of hopefuls about at the time. Anything to get on to the network: yes, and I mean anything!

'Hello, this is Ray Lakeland. I'm the BBC's Outside Broadcasts producer in the north, and I'm also responsible for *Come Dancing* in these parts. How'd you like to present the north's contribution next week from the Locarno, Bradford?'

Come Dancing? Locarno, Bradford? Did I want to, really? He sensed my hesitancy.

'Don't worry, boy', he said. 'We've got a pretty poor lot, doubt they'll make the next round, so you'll only have to do it once.'

'You're on', I said, resolving to bring a new literary dimension to the *Come Dancing* commentary. There must be *something* else to say apart from the fact that he's a sagger-maker's bottom knocker, and her mum sewed on all thirty thousand sequins by hand. I discovered there wasn't.

What is more, the Northern Dance team must have got wind of Ray's opinion of them. They performed like Trojans, had the longest run ever in the competition, and I had to go back to the Bradford Locarno four more times! The biggest boost I had, though, came from Granada Television, Manchester, the independent television company in the north-west. I've never ever worked for ITV, but I reckon they did more to consolidate my BBC career than anybody. I was asked to audition for their evening magazine programme *Scene* at 6.30 and had to let my BBC boss know I was going to attend because I needed a day off. When I came back, BBC Contracts rang: 'We'd rather you didn't go to Granada', the man said. 'I'd like to come and talk to you about a two-year contract.'

* * * * *

It is ironic that during 1963, and into the spring of 1964, only three years after all that unsuccessful door-bashing I'd done to get into the BBC, they were now coming to me to ask me to do all kinds of exciting programmes. The pattern of my professional life was beginning to take shape, and a very broad spectrum it covered. First there was *Grandstand,* in which I gave a regular match report from the north into the end of the programme. The horror was to discover that after you'd darted away from the match ten minutes before the end to avoid the crowds and make the regional studios in time, the score had moved in that time from 3-1 to 3-3, and you hadn't even seen the last two goals! Then there was current affairs, including election reports on exciting political swings and interviews with political figures, both local and national.

In football I remember an amazing night at Roker Park, Sunderland, and a replayed cup tie against Manchester United. The place was bulging. In fact there was nearly a major disaster. Those locked out were trying to climb in, gates were collapsing, and the injured were being hauled off to hospital. The BBC Sports Department from London were filming the match, then rushing chunks of film through processing and transmitting it as soon as possible after the match had finished, from the nearest regional studio, which was Newcastle. I wasn't doing the commentary but was asked to introduce the coverage, and wind up afterwards. I went to the match nevertheless. I thought it would help my presentation no end if I'd actually seen it. I avoided the chaos, and left just before the end to dart away up to Newcastle. The BBC was sending up a London editor: 'Name of Alan Hart', they said: to oversee the broadcasting operations. The name meant nothing to me then, but Alan and I were to live together professionally cheek by jowl through many a future *Grandstand*, Olympic Games, World Cup and a host of other major BBC sporting occasions.

I reached the studio safely. Of Alan Hart, whom I'd never met, there was no sign: nor was there of any film, either. Just me, that tiny studio and the engineers, waiting for something to happen and transmission time getting nearer and nearer. 'I'd better sort out an opening link to deliver', I thought, and sketched out in words the big occasion, the floodlit drama, the crowds, the panic and so on. Five minutes to go before transmission. I was beginning to sweat. With only a minute or two left the film came, with part of the match anyway, and some goals on it! It was laced into the machine, and the local producer and I agreed his cue to run it. Then the studio door burst open and this lanky, bean-pole of a man, six feet four if he was an inch, arms everywhere, hair all over the place, rushed in. 'Alan Hart', he said. 'We've got to write an opening link, and fast', he said.

'It's already done', says I, and almost before he could reply the titles ran and we were on the air. I delivered my opening, and we were safely into the first clip of the match. Alan came back in. 'Sorry I was late', he said. 'Pandemonium at Roker, couldn't get out. Anyway you seem to have been well prepared.' With five minutes of the film left, what I'd feared all along happened. Another goal had been scored and was being rushed back on another roll of film. 'Sorry', said Alan, 'we're in the land of no alternatives. There's only this one machine, and when this film has finished you'll just have to prattle on as best you can while we take it off and put the new roll on. We'll be as quick as we possibly can.'

Apprenticeship

That was the night I learned the essential lesson of always going into a programme prepared for anything, with more material than you think you'll need. Because I'd taken the trouble to go to the match I was able to give a full eyewitness account of an evening that, because of the injuries to spectators, had become a major news story as well as a football match. I happily bought the time Alan Hart needed to change his roll, and that night began a very happy professional relationship that's still working today. He is now the head of BBC TV's Sports Department.

I am frequently asked about my favourite football teams; though on *Grandstand* now, if I nod a head in one direction or another, I'm accused of bias and prejudice. Football supporters are by definition very partisan, and in their eyes we commentators often suffer accusations of favouritism which we don't deserve. I recently had a letter from a lady in Yorkshire who insists that when I say 'Leeds United' a sneer comes into my voice, though truly I've no great feeling one way or the other about Leeds, except to say I've enjoyed some very hospitable evenings at Elland Road.

On another occasion I was doing the teleprinter at twenty to five on *Grandstand,* and made a comment on a drawn cup tie in London between Millwall and Everton. In the post on the following Monday were two abusive letters, one from Merseyside and one from East London, each accusing me of making an uncomplimentary remark about his team!

I do, though, have a soft spot for Stoke since I was born there, and even when we moved to Oswestry I always went to see them play whenever I could, either with my father, or my Uncle Frank, who took me very often when I was a young lad. I can still reel off the team of those days after the war. Herod in goal, only a small chap too, Mould, McCue, were the full-backs, Frank Mountford, brother of George, was at right-half. And at centre-half, my hero, Neil Franklin. What an elegantly constructive player he was. Kirton was the other half-back. Outside-right? Who else, but the great Stanley Matthews. I've seen him reduce class full-backs to gibbering incompetence with his beautiful dribbling (why don't we use that lovely word any more?) and his astonishing speed over ten yards to draw himself clear of his opponent. At inside right was Antonio – remember him? George Rowlands was his real name, Antonio a middle name, but he was known only as Antonio, and was billed in the programme thus. At centre forward was Freddie Steele. The old leather ball could be heard thwacking against that bald head of his the length of the field. Baker and Ormston made up the left wing.

My other soft spot is for Sunderland. My love affair with them began with those days in the north-east where regularly on Saturdays I reported their efforts to get promotion back into the First Division. The day they did I was there, as Max Boyce says, and cried tears with fifty thousand other Roker football nut-cases. Trouble is, these days they can't seem to put together a team good enough to stay in the top grade.

Years later, Sunderland FC showed what a thoughtful lot they can be. In 1973, long after I'd left the north-east and gone to London, they got into the FA Cup Final as a Second Division team against mighty Leeds United; in itself a remarkable achievement. And all those years later an invitation came from the club to 'F. Bough and lady' to attend the party after the final was over. I said to Nest, 'They'll never beat Leeds at Wembley in a million years, but it would be nice to go to the party. We might see an old friend or two.' Well, it is fairy-tale history now that Sunderland did beat Leeds with that much replayed Ian Porterfield goal, and won the FA Cup. That party afterwards was a delight. They were all so shell-shocked they didn't know whether to laugh or cry. There on the table was that old, battered, familiar FA Cup and hardbitten old newspapermen from the north, like Charlie Summerbell of the *Daily Mirror* and Doug Weatherall of the *Daily Mail* kept touching it and stroking it just to reassure themselves it wasn't all a dream! Even as recently as the winter of 1980 they were thoughtful enough to invite me to the Sunderland centenary celebration.

By June 1964 I was in London. Another slice of the cake, one of the ones you never have any control over, had slotted into place. BBC Sports Department's regular midweek programme at the time was *Sportsview*. It was a sports magazine programme in the sense that it concentrated on film stories about famous sports personalities, liberally laced with action, but was also reflective and creative unlike the *Sportsnight* we have today which is largely tied to hard news and particular events. The presenter was Peter Dimmock, and his stamp was heavily on the programme – sharp moustache, Savile Row suit, cutaway collar and hard little tie-knot. He looked every inch the successful businessman. He was, too. Peter had risen to be the Head of the BBC's Outside Broadcasts group, and was responsible therefore for anything from a Cup Final to a royal wedding. It must have been very difficult for the editors and producers of *Sportsview,* who were in theory in charge of the programme, to have the boss working for them. His executive duties were gradually swamping his television appearances, and on one of his trips abroad, I was wheeled down from Newcastle to present *Sportsview* in his place. Naturally it was a great thrill, and I recognised it, too, as a terrific opportunity to break into network television for good. And that's what happened. I became the regular stand-in for Dimmock, and eventually in 1964, Bryan Cowgill, who was the Head of Sports Department, gave me a contract to work in sport from London. Peter retired from the screen to concentrate on being the boss, and I became *Sportsview*'s regular presenter.

* * * * *

In 1964 the BBC Sports Department was still in the throes of welding itself into a professional outfit that has since become the envy of television companies throughout the world. At times it was not a pleasant process, but if you believe the end justifies the means then the finished article is a testimony to the skills of the early pioneers. When I arrived the boss was Bryan 'Ginger' Cowgill. He and Paul Fox had laid the foundations, and they were both to rise to high office in the BBC (in turn they both became Controller of BBC-1, the Corporation's principal network, and eventually left to take top jobs in ITV with Thames and Yorkshire Television respectively).

To say that Ginger was competitive is putting it extremely mildly. A tough, uncompromising Lancastrian, he knew exactly what he wanted and surrounded himself with people who would give it to him. His method of selection was crude but effective. 'I don't work with rubbish', he'd say, and pruned out the dead wood ruthlessly. He simply leant on his staff, professionally, to find out what they were made of. In one of my early *Grandstand* programmes a new producer appeared – Brian Venner. His great ambition was to be confirmed in the job: all he ever wanted was to produce and direct *Grandstand,* and given his first opportunity he had to endure Ginger Cowgill's initiative test.

The Boy Scout movement has seen nothing like it. For four-and-a-half hours Venner had to endure a barrage of orders from the boss, who sat behind him at the back of the control gallery, firing verbal bullets non-stop. 'Cut to it!' 'Go on!' 'Oh, too late!' 'Bloody 'ell, what are you doing! Look, if you can't handle it, get out of that chair and let somebody in who can!' Venner hung on like grim death. 'You *must* listen to what the commentator is saying! Do I have to do everything round here?'

As the presenter, down on the studio floor, I could hear all this in the talkback line into my ear. By the time the programme was over, poor Brian Venner was a jelly, but just about intact. Ginger came into the studio. 'Well done', he said, 'bloody good programme'. I ventured to suggest that he'd given the producer a hell of an afternoon. 'Yes', he said, beamingly unrepentant. 'I thought he handled it very well. He'll do me.'

With Ginger, it was all straightforward and uncomplicated. You either produced the goods for him, or went away and worked somewhere else, and he wasted no time in finding out which course you were to follow. Brian Venner lived to hear the voice of the Clitheroe Kid, as Cowgill was called, for many years, and has become a great friend of mine and a television producer of the very highest class.

Cowgill was also fortunate to have David Coleman, who'd been the *Grandstand* presenter from the programme's beginnings in late 1958. By 1964, Coleman was in his pomp. Soon after I arrived in London I went along to White City to watch him link the programme from that stadium on the day of an athletics international. He not only held the programme together, moving smoothly from event to event, to racing, back to athletics, to football news, more racing, football results; he also commentated on the athletics international itself. His performance was an absolute *tour de force,* and all the time he had Ginger in his ear from the Lime Grove control gallery a mile down the road. Coleman set standards of broadcasting that enhanced the reputation of BBC TV Sports Department, and which the rest of us have since striven to build up.

When I arrived in London, all the talk was about the forthcoming Olympic Games. In 1964, the XVIIIth Games were to be held in Japan. For the first time an Asian country was to be the host. To my delight, and apprehension, I was included in the BBC's commentary team for Tokyo. I hadn't travelled outside Europe at the time, so an expenses-paid trip to the other side of the world was an exciting prospect. At the same time, I was very much aware that coming so early in my

Apprenticeship

network career, the 1964 Olympics were a golden opportunity of getting a quick foothold on the ladder to success – or disappearing without any further trace! So, to arm myself, I tried to find out what would be required of me. Just about anything and everything it seemed, since I was very much the apprentice, the junior member of the team. The 'heavyweights', like David Coleman and Harry Carpenter, had long since established their roles in athletics and boxing. So as far as I could see, I was to be used as a roving reporter, with a film crew, to preview the efforts of British competitors and foreign stars, and to follow up with interviews and features after they had succeeded or failed in their Olympian efforts.

There would be commentary jobs too, said Bryan Cowgill; there were indeed. I commentated on no fewer than six sports at those Games – wrestling, hockey, football, weightlifting, gymnastics, and the equestrian events. How I got away with it I'll never know. Once or twice, as the story unfolds, you'll probably agree, I didn't.

The memories are still vivid. To start with, on the journey out, by Comet, that loveliest, though cramped of old aeroplanes, I discovered a kindred soul. In the dark of the night crossing the continent of India, I found myself sitting alongside a young BBC radio commentator who, like me, was determined to earn his broadcasting spurs at those Tokyo Olympics. We shared with each other our hopes and our ambitions, and our determination not to be deflected by the fleshpots of Asia, by the night clubs and the bath-houses of the Ginza, Tokyo's West End, but to work hard and to give the pound and a half of flesh that the BBC demands on big international sporting occasions. His name was Brian Moore, and whether or not he succeeded in putting aside the temptation of the mystic Orient I've never asked him, but he's since become a highly respected and skilful broadcaster with Independent Television, succumbing there at least to the lure of the financial rewards of the London Weekend Company.

I do, on the other hand, remember being somewhat disappointed that the BOAC air stewardess on the Comet didn't quite live up to the expectations I had of being served by the incredibly smooth glamour girls that I'd always imagined crewed the large intercontinental jets. Indeed, the girl who attended to my needs on the flight, although personable enough, was rather a plain thing, to my regret.

Cue Frank!

But something happened on the trip that made me reflect on the marvellously attractive qualities of English women. You see, in Japan as you know the woman's role is a very subservient one. At least it certainly was in 1964, and I suspect that it has changed comparatively little ever since. To the Western male, it is a marvellous concept. Wherever you go, socially, a woman appears for each man, to do for him what the man would do for the woman in the West, for example help you into a chair, on with your coat, a light for your cigarette. On one extraordinary occasion, I remember leaving the table in the restaurant to go to the lavatory, to discover that my hostess was preceding me through the tables and leading the way to the loo. To do what I thought? Pull the chain? Help me with my zip? Wash my hands? The mind boggled. To my disappointment she merely opened the door for me, and I went in. To my astonishment, she was still outside the door when I came out again, waiting to show me back to the table. As well as looking after your every need they were, on the face of it, immensely agreeable companions, literally. 'Yes, sir; yes, sir, three bags full', was their motto. The man was always right, super, and beyond question. For a while, it's grand, but then how boring it becomes. You simply long for a good, spirited, independent-minded English girl to tell you you're talking a whole load of codswallop. Men can, you know, after a few jars, and saki has much the same effect on our arrogance and pomposity as gin and tonic! Therefore it was interesting to discover that after three weeks of this treatment, when I saw that plain English air stewardess stopping over at our hotel on another flight, she suddenly appeared the most marvellously interesting and attractive woman I'd ever seen . . .

While I'm on the subject of women, the 1964 Olympic Games were unique in being the only occasion to my knowledge that the BBC has ever booked its commentary team into a brothel! I discovered this three days into the trip while we were at a reception for the British Olympic team in the British Embassy, which was quite near to the hotel where we were staying. I was talking to the Third Secretary. 'Where are all you chaps from the BBC staying?' he asked. 'The Diamond Hotel', said I. He spluttered and went red. 'Really?' he said, 'most interesting'. After a few more glasses he revealed that the Diamond Hotel was particularly famous for the excellent quality of its room service, Japanese style. However, and I

Apprenticeship

can't quite remember fortunately who it was that found out, it later transpired that the Japanese in their efforts to clean up the city of Tokyo for the Games, and present an unsullied image to visitors from all over the world, had decided that the seamier activities of the hostess and bathroom trade would be suspended during the Games while the world's spotlight was upon them. This decision included the very special room service at the Diamond Hotel. But the Japanese do have very precise minds, and the phrase 'during the Games' meant precisely that. Their face-saving efforts were completely ruined when after the closing ceremony, with the Olympic flag lowered and the flame extinguished, the Diamond Hotel announced to us all as we collected our keys, that 'room service, sir, is now resumed'!

On the Tokyo trip it was brought home to me how rapidly the world is shrinking in size and how television was then beginning to hasten the process. I was in Hong Kong on the way to the Games. We had a one night stopover, a brief chance to sniff the atmosphere of a teeming, vibrant city. I was still agog with the pleasures of my first intercontinental flight, and my first acquaintance with the Orient. Hong Kong certainly lives up to everybody's idea of the East – it is warm, colourful, and noisy – and the hotel, the Miramar, certainly complemented the picture. I had a lovely room, a suite in fact, with a handsome carved screen separating bedroom from lounge. Carved figures decorated the tables, and exotic Ming-style lamps threw a warm, subdued light over all. I opened the shutters and breathed in the warm scented air and listened to new, unfamiliar sounds from the street below.

I then ruined everything, by switching on the television set to find Kenneth Wolstenholme commentating on a 'match of the day' between Leeds and Arsenal!

Is nowhere in the world safe from the box? I once had a letter from an ex-girlfriend, who had married a doctor and gone to live in the Shetland Islands. She wrote excitedly that the Islands had just got telly and that she'd seen me on the box, all the way from Lerwick, and wasn't it wonderful. I remember thinking, what a shame. There should be one or two places on earth where you can go without having Frank Bough thrust upon you. There should be places designated as areas of national peace and quiet, prohibited from television like the National Parks are from development!

At the Tokyo Games I was to have my first view of many

great Olympians. Five Olympics later, the roll call is long and distinguished, but I can revive the heroes of 1964 as in a videotape replay. For instance, Abebe Bikila, the Ethiopian marathon runner, who shouldn't have been there at all, let alone winning a gold medal: five weeks before his event, and remember it was the marathon, he'd had an operation for appendicitis. Two weeks later he was back in training, and by the day of the race he was fit enough to line up for a run of 26 miles 385 yards. A little over two hours later, he crossed the line four minutes ahead of Britain's Basil Heatley, and then proceeded to scorn the proffered blanket and lie down in the centre of the arena, winding down with an extraordinary display of bicycling exercises.

Then there was the American swimmer, Don Schollander, who won four gold medals and set three world records, beating Bobby MacGregor by a touch in the 100 metres. A boxer called Joe Frazier won the heavyweight boxing gold medal, and don't believe anyone who tells you that the popularity of gymnastics began with Olga Korbut. It had its real roots in Tokyo 1964, when a pretty blonde Czech, Vera Caslavska, won three gold medals.

Mary Rand (as she then was) won the long jump. I took her to an old Japanese market place in Tokyo to do some filming before her event. Her appearance in public was a sensation. She wore a white sweater and a pair of very brief white shorts, and with her head of blonde hair contrasting with the dark Japanese, she stood head and shoulders above the natives crowding around her. You could see that day, as she chatted and shopped and was everything to everybody, why they called her the golden girl of British athletics.

But the sharpest etching on my memory is of Ann Packer, winning the Olympic 800 metres gold medal. As it happened, she did so in a new world and Olympic record time of two minutes 1.1 seconds. I say 'as it happens' because if I could roll the slow motion replay now it would show much more than the satisfaction of that not inconsiderable achievement. As she timed her burst to perfection, and floated past Dupureur of France, the realisation dawned in the mind of Miss Packer that it had all been worthwhile. All that numbing, slogging training, all the sacrifice, all those months, even years of abstention from the pleasures of life, were reaping their reward and here and now, at this moment, in the Olympic Stadium in Tokyo. As she crossed the line, she seemed to look inward at herself, not out to the roaring stands around her, and a great serenity showed in her face, as visibly it relaxed and smiled. The worry of it all, the pressure of the days before, all fell away. She looked magnificent.

Throughout it all, Bough was keeping his end up – or trying to. By the middle of the second week of the Games, with the end in sight, I'd come to a brief moment of rest in the BBC Olympics office, and taking stock, I decided that although I hadn't set the airwaves alight, so far I was relatively un-scathed. I'd done commentaries on Olympic football, a game I knew well, and on hockey. (I'd played for Shropshire once or twice, which may sound an arrogant thing to say in print, but Shropshire is a relatively thinly-populated county, and if you owned a stick you were in the team almost. So it is no great boast, and my hockey-playing days as a youth certainly stood me in great stead in Tokyo.) I'd also done weightlifting, which is largely a question of identifying the competitor, grunting out loud with him when he got the bar above his head, and adding up the weights accurately – which I always found the most difficult part, figures never being one of my strong points.

Still to come, I thought, are the equestrian events, which are always at the end of the Games. I'd have to put some work in on that, since at the time my knowledge of the dressage and jumping business was nil. Heaven only knows why I was allocated them. Peter Dimmock had been going to do the show jumping but had decided to go home early. Shrewd fellow!

I've always found that at any time when I'm congratulating myself on keeping my head above water, that's the moment when the proverbial hits the fan, and it did then.

I was aroused from my reverie by Leslie Kettley, the producer in charge of the camera team with which I'd been darting around, doing interviews and follow-ups between my various commentaries.

'Right', he said, 'get yourself out to the Budokai Hall where Denis McNamara could win an Olympic medal in two hours time'.

'Denis who?' I asked. 'What does he do?'

'McNamara is a Greco-Roman wrestler', said Les, 'and right out of the blue he's come through from the preliminary rounds and this afternoon fights a Magyar. If he wins it's a bronze medal at least, and the opportunity of a silver or even better.'

In no time flat I was in the camera car with Roy Gladish – a marvellous cameraman with whom I've worked many times since, and with a lot of fun too – belting out to the suburbs of Tokyo. 'Roy', I said, 'this is it. Never heard of Denis McNamara, know absolutely nothing about Greco-Roman wrestling – it's curtains!'

Roy was already hardened to the challenges of the unexpected. 'Look', he said, 'I've got to find a camera position when we get to this place. While I'm doing that, why not have a word with the British official at the venue. There's bound to be one there if McNamara is on the mat, and he'll at least be able to give you a potted biography of the bloke and if you are lucky one or two of the basic rules of the sport.'

We arrived and bluffed our way in. That was difficult with the Japanese, who always wanted to see the right piece of paper, and since Denis McNamara had not been on our forecast list of British successes, that we hadn't got.

Roy disappeared to find somewhere for the camera, and sure enough I discovered a blazered British official and introduced myself.

'My name's Frank Bough', I said, 'BBC Television. We've come to cover Denis McNamara's big moment.'

He was delighted, as all minority sport devotees are, at the prospect of their favourite pastime enjoying for once the full light of worldwide publicity. 'Terrific', he said. He's won his last preliminary bout this morning in splendid style and if he beats the Hungarian he . . .'

I interrupted, 'Yes', I said, 'he gets a bronze medal at least'.

'My word', he said admiringly, 'you are well up with events'.

My God, little did he know how little I knew. He was about to find out.

'Tell me', I said, 'I'm a bit short on biographical details on Denis', assuming an easy familiarity with the lad I'd never even seen, let alone seen wrestle.

'Ah yes', answered the blazer, 'well he's a South London policeman from Tooting Bec, has five children, and all his mates in the force have contributed to the expense of sending him to the Games, and they must be very proud of him'.

I took it all down. Then I had to hit him with the cruncher.

'Tell me something about Greco-Roman wrestling', I said casually.

His face dropped. 'You're kidding', he said. 'We have here the finest-ever prospect of an Olympic medal for British Greco-Roman wrestling, and the BBC send someone to cover the great moment, who knows nothing at all about the sport? You *are* from the BBC?' he asked disbelievingly.

'Look, I'm sorry', I said, 'but you have caught us with our pants down rather, and in any case I'm all you've got so a bit of help could benefit us all.'

He was furious. 'It's ridiculous – the boy's on the mat in half an hour. How can I tell you anything in that time about a highly sophisticated sport? You get marks for style, for good defence, for aggression, a whole host of inanimate skills I couldn't begin to tell you about in half an hour. You'll have to take a look at that', thrusting the daily programme into my hand, 'it's got a few pointers about the sport on the inside cover. Read them. It's all you'll have time for. And bloody good luck', he growled acrimoniously, as he stomped off.

Roy Gladish, meanwhile, had set up his camera in a gangway halfway up a huge bank of seats. I sat three steps down below his camera and tried to sort myself out. The Budokai Hall was a beautiful, new, indoor arena, absolutely packed with five thousand devotees of Greco-Roman wrestling, any one of whom was better equipped to do a commentary on what was about to happen than I was. All attention was focused on a large blue mat in the centre of the arena floor. Suddenly I was caught up with the excitement. It was a strange feeling, not knowing what was going on, but being aware that something rather special was happening. After all, this was the Olympic Games, the best in the world, whatever the sport, and however specialist it was.

I'd no more time to think, because it all began to happen. The two contestants came on to the mat and I caught my first sight of Denis McNamara. 'All right for you', I thought, 'but what about poor old me?' I recollect that the introductions had a ceremonial all their own. The contestants were named, the crowd roared, the two men came to the centre of the mat, bowed to each other, shook hands, and returned to the edge of the mat. Three steps above and behind me, I heard Roy say 'I'm rolling, you can go ahead when you like'. With the huge crowd now silent, the two men faced each other in the middle of the blue mat, arms hanging at the ready, and began to circle each other warily.

I lifted the microphone to my lips and began. 'What a turn up for the books', I said, 'here in the Budokai Hall in faraway Tokyo, Denis McNamara has fought his way to a possible medal-winning position in the Olympic Greco-Roman wrestling competition. If he beats this Hungarian he wins an Olympic bronze medal.'

The two men continued to circle each other.

'Denis', I went on, 'is a South London policeman from Tooting Bec, with five kids, and all his mates have contributed to help send him to these Games. How proud of him they'll be today.'

I tell you, those two fellows did me no favours at all. They just shuffled round and round each other, looking for an opening. It seemed to me it could go on like this forever. By now I had delivered every single fact I knew about Denis McNamara's life and hard times, and I was getting desperate. I'm rather ashamed to tell you what I said next.

'For those of you who are not too familiar with this ancient sport of Greco-Roman wrestling, let me give you one or two pointers to look out for' – and I proceeded to read almost verbatim the inside cover of the programme that the blazer had given me.

At last the two wrestlers came to my aid. There was a tremendous collision of flesh on the mat, the crowd went wild, and at last I had something to shout about. I went bananas.

'He's got him! I think McNamara's got him. What a throw.'

There was pandemonium. Wrestlers heaving away, crowd roaring, me screaming like a madman and then suddenly, just as quickly as the action had started, it all stopped. The two men slowly disentangled themselves, got to their feet, bowed politely to each other, put on their robes and – just went. I sat there, microphone to open mouth, a classic case of professional *coitus interruptus*.

I crushed the microphone to my sleeve, where it wouldn't pick up the sound, and turned to Roy Gladish, three steps above me. His right eye was still firmly attached to his viewfinder.

'Roy', I shouted.

'Yup', he replied.

'Roy, do you, er, reckon they're finished, Roy?'

'Yup', he said, somewhat sympathetically, since the large blue mat was by now absolutely empty. 'Yup – I reckon they've finished.'

'Roy?' I said again.

'Yup', he said.

'Roy, who d'you reckon won, Roy?'

'I'm buggered if I know', he replied.

Apprenticeship

And there we were, the pair of us, representing the finest television system in the world, and neither of us knew if Mr McNamara had won his bronze medal or not.

It was, I'm sure, no consolation to Denis, but in the fullness of time, it was a great relief to me to discover that he'd lost and that awful commentary never saw the light of day . . .

I had an equally narrow escape the following day when I tackled the equestrian events, the very last part of my first Olympic schedule. Dressage, you may know, is really for the *aficionados* – beautiful to watch, with horse and rider reaching for a complete understanding, one with the other, but it is damnably difficult to understand. The series of precise, controlled movements are really comprehensible only to the select few who adjudicate the dressage events. I remember two things – that I had the invaluable help of Slim Wilkinson, one of the department's most senior and experienced producers, who sat alongside me throughout a very long day. In fact, we were all so clapped out by the end part of the Games, that Slim spent most of the non-commentary periods fast asleep beside me. We also decided that in order to make a decent showing, we had to pull together as a real team, so to add to the preparation I'd already done in an effort to understand the dressage, Slim bought a daily programme, in which were written the sequence of delicate, difficult movements horse and rider had to perform.

We got on famously: as each horse went through its paces, Slim pointed out the particular movement, and I'd identify it through the microphone. We got so cocky that after a while I decided I'd count, on air, the eight flying changes, as one sequence is called.

'Now', I said, after the fashion of the poor man's Dorian Williams, 'we come to the flying changes. Let's count them for you. One, two, three, four five, six –.' At this point horse and rider broke off and went into another movement. 'Well, there you are, those were the flying changes!'

Always recognise your limitations, was a lesson I learnt that day.

Actually I must have got away with it reasonably successfully, apart from the fact that when I got home, Nest, who is a horsewoman, said I'd done splendidly at the dressage, until I'd referred to a beautiful grey horse as 'that white horse over there'!

3
DIGGING IN

For me, reporting the Tokyo Olympic Games was really being thrown in at the deep end. When the Games were over, I rose to the surface again, spluttering and blowing a bit – but at least I'd survived.

When I came home I really started to dig in. In a way, the next few years were the most varied I have ever enjoyed, either before or since. Although in the seventies I was to return very happily to news and current affairs (and I can think of no one else currently in television who gets both a political interview with a prime minister and a Cup Final through his hands), those sporting sixties were a tremendous experience. Much of the work was done on location, and I travelled all over Europe and America.

For a while, the centre of my life was *Sportsview,* one of the Sports Department's original programmes, and for my money one of the best. As I have said, it was a magazine programme, sweet and simple. It didn't cover sporting events only as events, but also reported them through the eyes of the competitors, examined their history, and the politics of them. In fact, although the idea of a magazine programme is sometimes belittled, the great joy is that you can put into it whatever you like. There are no boundaries.

Grandstand, of course, is the great events programme. It is about action, fast-moving pictures, horses tearing across the screen, motor cars roaring in every direction, sixes being struck in top-class cricket. There is a pace about *Grandstand* which dictates that a slow, quiet, thoughtful piece of reporting is really quite out of place. But in *Sportsview,* each Wednesday, for thirty-five minutes or so you could vary the pace, and change gear in much the same way we do in *Nationwide,* another 'magazine' programme. There was room for, say, an action report on the Monaco Grand Prix, well shot on film the previous Sunday, well cut for the best pictures,

46

with me diving around the pits getting lap by lap reaction from drivers and mechanics, as well as a background piece shot on the Berkshire downs, about the training and preparation of a great racehorse.

If there's one thing I'm grateful to *Sportsview* for, it is that it taught me how to water-ski. I went to film the British Championships on a gravel pit at Sonning in Berkshire. In Britain, water-skiing was a cinderella sport. The climate is lousy for it, and world champions tended to come from Italy and France and Florida, where they could practise in warm, still water in sunny conditions. Happily for British water-skiing, a man called David Nations had other ideas – the dream of a British world champion. Nations's energy, his wild optimism, his ability to talk the hindlegs off a donkey if it would help his sport, did the trick, and in Mike Hazelwood his dream came true when Hazelwood won the world title in Milan in 1978.

At that Sonning gravel pit in 1967, all that was in the future, and to most people (other than David Nations) just pie in the sky.

The producer who was working on the film with me was Bob Abrahams, a delightfully aggressive little Londoner. He has a great love of sport, a fine knowledge of what a film camera can do, and, what's more, a fertile mind that was constantly thinking up new ways of how reporters should operate.

'I've had this great idea, Frank', he said, 'of you opening the film report, saying where we are and what we are doing, while you're being towed along on a pair of skis'.

'You're mad', I replied. 'I can't water-ski – end of message.'

To Bob, that was a minor problem. 'Well you'd better bloody well learn, hadn't you?'

He has a way with him, does Abrahams. The day before the filming we went along to Sonning, and met David Nations. The idea didn't seem to be a problem to him, either.

'We'll have you up and going in no time, lad', he said airily. 'We've got this great new idea' (Nations has great new ideas at the rate of about one every hour of his waking life, and some I suspect while he's fast asleep) 'of how to get youngsters skiing well, and quickly. You see, the problem has always been getting up on the skis and moving. It puts a lot of people off when they can't make it after several attempts. Trouble is you tell 'em to push down with their legs, to use them like motor car shock absorbers and to keep their arms absolutely stiff and straight when they rise from the water – and then they take off and forget it all, and go pulling and heaving the rope all over the place and down they go. We've cracked that one though. We've got this extra long towing bar that'll take two people at once, so the instructor can ski alongside the pupil and put him right as they go along.'

Confronted with such unquenchable enthusiasm, what could I do? Somebody poured me into a wet suit, slotted my feet into a pair of skis, and I flopped into the water.

The first problem, of course, is to adopt that curious foetal position – sitting in the water, arms outstretched, with the skis almost vertical in front of you and the tips sticking out by your nose, the rope lying between them. Achieving that successfully is really difficult, because in the water the skis have a mind of their own. The water pressure pushes them this way and that so they won't come upright, and as for the rope, that's everywhere but where you want it! But I eventually managed it. 'Right', says the instructor. 'Hold the bar very tightly, because when the towing boat accelerates there's quite a pull.' Too right. Off went the boat, my arms came out of their sockets, and the towing rope went winging away across the water.

One more time I tried. 'If you manage to hang on', said the instructor, 'do remember to push down on the skis and keep your arms straight on your rise'. I hung on, and, miracle of miracles, began to lift towards the surface of the lake. But I hadn't listened, had I? As my chest lifted free of the water pressing on it, I had this overwhelming desire to heave on the bar. My somersault was highly spectacular and worth about 8.2 marks!

But I got up in the end, and there I was, stuttering across the gravel pit. Admittedly I didn't look too elegant, but I hung on like grim death, really enjoying the wonderfully intoxicating feeling that water-skiing gives you. My enjoyment lasted about twenty seconds. Nobody had told me about the wash of the boat. If you're moving straight forward, you're skiing in smooth water between the wash caused by the towing boat; but sooner or later the boat has to turn, and the skier has to cross a ridge of turbulent water. Well, this one didn't. Skier, skis and boat suddenly moved in three separate directions and the world turned over several times.

An hour and several duckings later, I climbed into the boat, and returned to the shore. From top to toe, muscles I didn't even know I had were complaining like mad, and I had also swallowed copious quantities of water.

Bob was still determined. 'You can do it, lad' he said. 'I'll call the crew for tomorrow morning.'

'Where'll the camera be?' I asked.

'Oh, in the towing boat, pointing back at you. It'll be a terrific shot.'

'And the radio microphone?' I said.

That apparently had to be round my neck, as an additional hazard. I could end up throttled and drowned simultaneously.

'I've been thinking about that' said Bob. 'Keeping the water out is the problem, but the engineers have been working on the idea of enclosing it in a plastic bag. They reckon they'll be able to waterproof it to enable you to get up on to the skis, but if you fall off then it'll be a write off.'

'But I *always* fall off!' I pointed out.

'So?' he said. 'It's a one-take job. You'll have to get it right, words and all, first time. There'll be no second chance.'

Charming. All this, plus prize-winning prose as well.

The following morning we put it all together. The camera was set in the boat, and the radio microphone hitched round my neck. The engineers had made a very neat job of the plastic bag, but obviously the top of the mike into which my words would go had to remain clear. Oh, and the transmitter, by the way, was in another waterproof bag strapped to my back, out of sight. With all that, as well as a pair of skis, I looked ready for a moonshot.

I slid into the water. Must hold my position. Push down with the feet. Mustn't pull at the rope. Remember the words.

Suddenly I was up and moving. The towing boat looked somewhat chaotic, packed to the gunnels with driver, cameraman, sound recordist and Bob, waving his arms about to indicate they were rolling. I straightened up, tried to look as though I'd been water-skiing all my life, drew breath, and launched into my prose.

'Welcome to *Sportsview*, which starts with a report on water-skiing, very much a minority sport in Britain at the moment, but one that's attracting an ever-growing army of devotees. Here at Sonning in Berkshire, they're holding the British Water-Skiing Championships and it's hoped that one day we'll produce somebody of world class who can take on the top performers from the warmer climates of the European mainland.'

Cue Frank!

I was concentrating so hard on getting the words out properly that I didn't notice we'd run out of gravel pit, and the boat driver was having to turn in a big arc. I was giving the words full throat when my left ski hit the wash, and over I went in my most spectacular somersault to date, still talking as I sank beneath the waves. On the film there were two great gurgles and a swishing noise and then silence as the water flooded into the microphone. Still, it made an excellent programme opening! I think they threw the mike away.

The advent of radio microphones sent film producers into ecstasy. The fact that you could dispense with a piece of wire connecting speaker to recording machine opened up a million new ways of using the reporter. He was asked increasingly to perform deeds of derring-do, because sound meant one could really eavesdrop on a sportsman and find out what it was like to do what he did.

After the water-skiing, my next assignment was to sit in a two-man bob, and go down the St Moritz bob run talking about what it was like on the way. That was all well and good, but the second man in a two-man bob has to do the braking, however good the driver is. I had a very good one – a great Swiss champion, Nino Bibbia, who was also a great Cresta champion. That's the run in St Moritz where you travel down what is basically a saucer-shaped track, on a tiny sled – head first, lying on your stomach, and braking with the tips of your toes. I'm sure there are crazier methods man has devised to amuse himself in sport, but I can't think of one off-hand! However, this was the bob.

Nino gave me my instructions. During the ride, I was to hold the two brake handles, each side of the bob, and when he shouted 'Brake!' I was to apply a steady pressure upwards so that the teeth of the brake bar would grip smoothly.

This time I was dressed up in crash helmet, heavy anorak and trousers, plus of course microphone and transmitter. The first thing for which I was totally unprepared was the noise. The run is made of ice, so the clatter of the metal runners against the floor is deafening. The other alarming development was the fear that in all the banging and clattering, I wouldn't hear Nino's instructions to brake. I was convinced that I'd failed to hear him, when I looked forward over his shoulder and saw the run ending in what appeared to be a solid wall of ice. That was the first sweeping wall of the run, as it cornered off to the right. We were upon it before Nino shouted 'brake' and I jerked convulsively at the two handles – I'd forgotten all about steady pressure by this time.

All this time I was talking my head off, trying to give my own thoughts as to what the experience was like. When we played the tape after the run was finished, my voice sounded completely terror-stricken. It was! But I wouldn't have missed the experience, though.

The bob-run film was part of a longer report which constituted the whole of a *Sportsview* programme on the celebrations to mark a hundred years of winter sport in St Moritz. It was a fabulous four days. I'd never been to a winter sports resort before, and St Moritz is a fairy-tale village, a complete mixture of local colour and extreme sophistication. All the smart Paris stores have a branch there, at the top of the Engadine valley, and yet when you travel on the little single-track train that heaves you up from Chur at the bottom, you'd never think there could be anything at the top. The view is magnificent as the train winds its way through rugged mountain passes and forest, with the valley first on one side and then on the other.

There's a delightful story about how St Moritz first became a winter sports resort back in 1867. Whether it's true or not, it is difficult to say, but the locals certainly encourage it. One of the most famous of the hotels is the Kulm Hotel, which has been in the Badrutt family for generations. In the 1860s the patron was Johannes Badrutt, and during the summer months his hotel was patronised by rich English landed gentry who spent their holidays there. One autumn, when he was bidding a party of them farewell, he said: 'I can't understand why you always go back to London for the winter. They tell me the fogs are terrible and the weather is so dark, cloudy and cold. Up here in the Swiss mountains the sun shines from a cloudless sky, it is warm, and the air is crisp and bubbles like champagne.'

'Rubbish, Herr Badrutt', they said. 'You can't be serious.'

'Well', said Johannes, 'I'll tell you what I'll do. I'll make a wager with you. Come back to St Moritz in January when the English fogs are at their worst and if it isn't as I say it is here, you can stay at the Kulm for a week as my guests.'

The English took him at his word, convinced they were going to have a free holiday, and in January they set off up the Engadine valley from Chur. It was cloudy and raining. They agreed they were mad, but at least Johannes would look after them well. Higher and higher they went, still in cloud, and then just before they reached St Moritz the little train broke through it. The sky was blue and there was deep snow everywhere, exactly as Johannes had said. And there he was, greeting them at the door of the Kulm, beaming broadly, in his shirtsleeves.

The English were so delighted with the weather, so the story goes, that they devised ways of amusing themselves in this strangely beautiful climate – and winter sport in St Moritz was born. Anyway, the locals are so convinced all this is true that they were busy celebrating the centenary of Johannes Badrutt and his famous wager in 1867, as I made my debut on the bob.

For me it was a time of firsts, as I burrowed my way into the television scene, trying all the time to learn good professional habits. I made my first trip to America, and attended my first Cup Final (because although I'd played at Wembley in the University match, I'd never been to see a big game there), and my first motor racing grand prix.

Sportsview sent me to cover Monaco with Roy Gladish (whom you will remember from that Greco-Roman wrestling incident at the Tokyo Olympics) as cameraman. The idea was to get the best possible pictures of the race on film, as well as tell the story of the event: how the lead changed, who were the leading contenders, who fell out and why. Gladish really was an ace with the pictures. One camera position I remember particularly. He'd park himself on the pavement just outside the famous tunnel near the harbour, find a good place for his camera on the kerb and press the button, with the car wheels screaming by inches from the lens. They were dramatic shots, taken so low, and I never did see anybody down there but Roy.

My job was to stay in the pits during the race, keeping track of how the race was going so that I could write my script over Roy's pictures ready for transmission the following Wednesday. If Brabham or Hill or Jim Clark came into the pits, there was always the chance of a quick word into the microphone before they roared off again back into the race.

I first met Graham Hill at that Monaco Grand Prix. The crowds adored him. He had a habit of winning there, and they liked the style of the man, his bravado, and his approachability. Graham always had a moment for you. Life for him was now, in the present, and he was very keen to admire the view as he lived it.

Digging In

I remember attending a private dinner once of drivers, engineers and journalists, after the presentation of the Ferodo Trophy, awarded each year to the person who is considered to have given most to motor sport that year. On recollection, the evening may appear rather undergraduate, all rather 'lads together'. It certainly wasn't the kind of party that would have won any votes from Germaine Greer: it was very male chauvinist piggy, but the most tremendous fun, and as ever Graham Hill was the powerhouse of the occasion! The host had engaged a couple of strippers, one of whom appeared in the centre of the floor (it was only a small private room, with about fifty or so of us at dinner) carrying a large wicker basket. As she went through her act, Graham's role was that of commentator, and he had everyone in stitches. But this time, he'd taken on the wrong lady. After putting up with his remarks for a while, she smiled sweetly, dug into the wicker basket and came up with a large, sleepy boa constrictor, which she proceeded to wind round Graham's neck! I can tell you, the place went very quiet indeed.

But, although the lady had made her point, she hadn't quiet finished. After the snake had been returned to the basket and everyone had relaxed, including Graham, who was in full flow again with the wisecracks, our entertainer felt it necessary to assert her position once again. With the speed of light, she slipped a revolver from the basket, stuck it between Graham's legs and fired. Graham's face went ashen, he leapt up, quickly turned away – and got the second barrel up his backside. The lady had won, game, set and match!

Mind you, he couldn't have been an easy man to live with, darting all over the world as he did. I'm certain Betty, his wife, rode the occasional emotional roller-coaster as life went by. She is an admirable woman, and I think without her Graham might well have sunk without trace. I recall being on holiday with the family in Portugal one year, and surfacing a hundred yards off the Algarve coast to find Betty Hill swimming alongside me. She'd managed to pin Graham down long enough to join her and the children at Luz Bay. They were marvellously hospitable, and wanted to be introduced to our three sons, whom they'd never met, asked us round for drinks and supper, and finally Graham autographed a photograph for each of the lads. He did everything like that so well.

Alan Hart, when he was editor of *Grandstand,* and I went to see Graham in hospital after he'd had a terrifying car crash at

Watkins Glen. At the time they were busily reassembling the lower half of his body with bolts and pins. 'That's it' they told him. 'No more motor racing for you. You've survived by the skin of your teeth. Be thankful, and when we've lashed you together again you can be the Grand Old Man of British motor racing and go and open fetes and things.' 'I've told 'em bollocks!' he said to us. He fought his way back on to his feet again, finding time in the process to discover that three-wheeler invalid cars were dangerously unstable and wage a ferocious campaign to have them put right. Many was the time he'd come hammering on the *Nationwide* door: 'Why don't you do a piece about these three-wheelers, they're a bloody menace.'

Miraculously, he did drive again, though I suspect there was a slight conspiracy in the motor racing world to prevent Graham Hill from driving a car that was so fast he might kill himself. I last saw him limping down Dover Street in the West End of London. 'Boughy, I'm glad I've seen you – I've got to do something for this boys' club – wonder if you'd come along one night and . . .'

But at that first Monaco of mine in the sixties I also met the other Graham Hill – a very professional man, very knowledgeable about his car and what he could ask it to do. Very British he was, too; Graham really did see himself as an ambassador for his country. And he was certainly that. I first set eyes on him as he walked down the pit straight to his car on the grid with the other drivers, smiling, waving at the packed stands in the warm May sunshine. It was very moving, very exciting, in a way gladiatorial, because everywhere was an unspoken acknowledgement that those drivers were in the ring, tilting at death itself. Indeed, that very day one young driver made that walk for the last time. I was at the Ferrari pit when word came through that Italy's Lorenzo Bandini had burned himself to death when his car struck an obstacle and exploded down by the harbour. The mechanics sat and wept unashamedly. Admire the view in life while you can: it was impossible to deny Graham Hill's philosophy and when he crashed his plane trying to land in fog in Hertfordshire I knew he was right. I shed a tear that day too.

There were trips across the Atlantic, too. I was asked to go to America to make a film about football – soccer. Phil Woosnam, the Welsh International player, had been appointed to run the Atlanta Braves, and help encourage the growth of the new National Football League. The stadium was unbelievable. 'Built in a year flat' said the mayor proudly. I went to Mexico, to assess the problems of having the 1968 Olympic Games at 7,500 feet. 'There are some who will die' said a Swedish coach. Nobody did, but a long jumper called Bob Beaman rocketed through the thin air to jump 29 feet 2½ inches. The previous world record was 27 feet odd, so he'd leapt over the 28 feet mark completely.

I also found time to be a football commentator as well, doing regular commentaries for *Match of the Day*. And of course in 1966, the World Cup Finals in England really set the pattern of televised football, with panels of experts and the early slow motion machines, very Heath Robinson, but excitingly new, being cranked up to show grainy black and white action replays. I was dispatched to my old stomping ground in the north-east to cover the group matches in Sunderland, Middlesbrough and Newcastle. Two of the countries playing there, Russia and Chile, did little to stir the blood but there was Italy (at that time at the low end of the pendulum of manic depression that all Italian football teams are heir to, despite having some wonderful players in their team), and there were the North Koreans. They had emerged from the Far East qualifying group and we were all rushing about trying to find out something about them. I remember going to a training session with a list of their names, which, by the way, were a commentator's nightmare. Pak Do Ik and Pang Seung Jim and the like.

Now, when I prepared homework for a football commentary I'd lay out the names of the teams on a large sheet of paper, facing each other in the position they were due to play. Alongside each name I'd enter his record, all the facts and figures I might need during the commentary, and of course, most important, his number so that if there was any danger of misidentification I could quickly look down and check. I'd prepare another sheet in precisely the same way for the second half, with the teams on my sheet changing ends with the teams on the pitch in front of me. All of that was very much an aide mémoire as far as pure identification was concerned, because in the Western world players look different. There are short busy ones, like Alan Ball, there are toothless ones like Nobby Stiles, there are blond-headed ones like Bobby Moore and there are black ones like Pele and Eusebio. No problems. When I saw the North Koreans I swallowed very hard indeed. They all looked exactly alike! Height five feet six. Build slight. Complexion oriental with narrow eyes. Hair dark, close-cropped. Every single one of the squad looked as though he had been stamped out of a machine.

The football commentator's nightmare is to get the goal-scorer wrong, and truly it can be very difficult to decide who poked the ball in from a crowded goal-mouth scramble. And the commentator has to get it right and get it right immediately. No time to pause and lick the pen as they do in press boxes. *Daily Express* says to *Daily Mail:* 'Keegan, do you reckon, or did Heighway get a boot to it?' 'I thought it was Case' says *Telegraph*. They arrive at a mutual decision and just to be safe, somebody goes into the dressing room area at half-time for confirmation of who did score the goal.

No such luxury for David Coleman: 'Keegan' he's got to say. 'One-nil', and straight away. All this was running through my head as I watched these twenty-two identical North Koreans going through their training routine. I made one very quick and obvious decision. Nobody was going to get a mention unless he turned his back and showed me his number. Then another quite comforting thought struck me: who was to say I was wrong, anyway!

The little men became the darlings of the local north-east supporters, who latched on to their furiously energetic style of play. They never stopped. Busy, busy, busy, running, running, everywhere, little legs going like the clappers for all ninety minutes. Their opponents were given no peace whatsoever. What a night it was when they played the Italians: Italy, the sophisticates of European football – elegant, skilful, decadent even, in the way they sometimes waste their immense talents.

I don't really think the North Koreans knew any of this. If they did, it didn't show. They went buzzing straight at the Italians, who just couldn't take it. It was nothing to do with skill, class, footballing genius – they'd that in abundance – but all to do with character and the mind. When Pak Do Ik scored the only goal of the match (I need hardly say that he was a North Korean) Ayresome Park went wild.

'What on earth has gone on here tonight' I said, as the demoralised Italians crept off at the end of the match. It was a wonderfully mystifying experience.

When the group games ended, my commentating duties did

Digging In

so too, and I was able to follow the rest of the competition and go to the final itself without worrying about work. That's a luxury that I've rarely enjoyed since. Of course it's marvellous to present a Cup Final or a Grand National, go to Lord's for the cricket World Cup Final and to Cardiff Arms Park for Wales/England and be in the middle of everything. Nevertheless, it's work, and a television programme is a worrying beast from start to finish, particularly if it is live. Every second there's an opportunity passing your nose to be lost or taken, and no chance of a retake. At the end of it, you look at all the good things you did and they're in one hand. The facts were right, the presentation neat with no rough edges showing – a clean programme we call it, free from verbal or technical error, the changing situation was recognised and properly ridden, and editorially the right decisions were made as the programme progressed. In the other hand, dammit, are the ones that got away. The interview we didn't get. The piece of important news that was inadvertently left out. The video-tape run that didn't happen. You resolve you'll do better next time! So to get to the World Cup Final between England and West Germany just to enjoy the match was a rare, relaxing pleasure indeed, particularly as the match ebbed and flowed, with England winning gloriously in extra time.

I enjoyed a quite extraordinary sequel to the match. Getting away from Wembley in a car after a big match is always a slow business so I joined a few colleagues in a nearby hotel to have a drink and toast England's success. After a decent interval I went to my car and drove off. Shortly I found myself, quite by accident, the car in the victory cavalcade next to the bus which carried the England players. I've seen nothing like it apart from a Coronation and dim memories of VE Day. The car horns were tooting away in unison, South American style, the pavements were packed with cheering crowds, and every window, balcony and vantage point bulged with people, cheering, singing, waving Union Jacks. All the way from Wembley to the West End, England's success was roared from the rooftops. It was a very warming experience.

A year later I was back at Wembley again – this time to work. At least that was the instruction. Chelsea were playing Spurs in an all-London Cup Final and my role was to do the beginning of *Grandstand* interviews on the morning of the match with Bill Nicholson and the Spurs team, and then to go to Wembley to stand by if needed for further duties.

Cue Frank!

Understandably, a football manager in the last few hours before a Cup Final is in a pretty edgy mood. There's a big prize to be won, kudos and financial reward for him and his players, and he wants nothing to upset the mood of his players, before the big game. So the Cup Final morning interviews on *Grandstand* are always a delicate affair, although some managers feel that to chat away merrily to the watching viewers does give the players something to do in those last few hours before the game, and actually helps to relax them.

Bill Nicholson, the Spurs manager, never seemed to me entirely happy about his players going through the motions on Cup Final morning, so mindful of my responsibilities, I sought him out on the Friday evening, just to check with him that he was still agreeable, though reluctant, and to try and reassure him we'd be as little trouble as possible.

The Spurs team were staying in the Mayfair Hotel, right in the middle of London's West End, which was a bit unusual. On the whole managers like to take their squads right away to some secluded country hotel with a few acres and a large fence round it, just to be sure that in the few days before the final their players are totally removed from all temptations of the flesh and of the boozer.

But the manager of the Mayfair was a Spurs fan through and through and knew Bill Nicholson well, and really looked after the welfare of his team like a broody hen. So careful was he that the players should not be upset by the slightest thing, he'd actually put notices up in all their bedrooms saying 'On no account drink the tap water! Bottled spring water is provided'. He was taking not the remotest chance that any of the players might be upset, and this in the most sophisticated and expensive square mile in Britain!

I waited and waited for the chance to have a word with Nicholson, and managed to catch him in the lobby. He was taking his players to the cinema, and then early to bed. Our conversation lasted all of thirty seconds. He didn't seem too enthusiastic about the idea, but it had all been agreed beforehand and he supposed it would be all right, but he'd see in the morning. Still, I'd made my gesture. Off Spurs went. The hotel manager on the other hand couldn't have been more accommodating and he was to play a considerable part in making that Cup Final for me a very pleasant one indeed. 'All OK?' he said. 'Well', said I, 'I've done all I can to see the interviews tomorrow go as well as possible'.

Digging In

'Right then' he said. 'Come down to the Beachcomber and have a bite to eat.' The Beachcomber is the Mayfair Hotel's seafood restaurant. If you like fish, particularly shellfish, it's a delight, and the setting does all it can to convince you that you're in the South Seas, with Hawaiian music in the air and saronged waitresses everywhere. Ate well that night, I did! The following morning I rose early, preparing myself for a tricky piece of work with Bill Nicholson and the team, but like all worries in life, when you actually confront them they never appear as horrific as they do in anticipation. Although Bill was not exactly a bundle of joy all went well, and the players seemed to enjoy it immensely.

When I'd finished, a message came through to me from the BBC control van outside in the street, that I was no longer needed at Wembley that afternoon and please could they have back the pass I'd got because they wanted it to give to a visiting official of the European Broadcasting Union.

So I went to say goodbye to the manager of the Mayfair Hotel, to thank him for being so helpful to me and the camera team. 'You're off to the match then?' he said. 'Well I was going' I said. 'But I'm no longer needed there, and my BBC working pass has been given to somebody else.' Now you can imagine how scarce a Cup Final ticket was for that match. They always are like gold, whoever's playing, but that year, with two London teams facing each other at Wembley, everybody in the capital wanted one. So what happened next was like fairyland. 'Well' he said . . . fishing into his waistcoat pocket. 'Try that one – you should get a good view' and into my right hand popped a stand ticket. 'And by the way' he said, 'you know the best way to Wembley is by public transport from Marylebone station – here's a return ticket to Wembley Park station. I always send one of my staff to buy a few early in the morning on Cup Final day. Saves you queueing when the crowds are thickest.' And before I could react to his generosity he looked at his watch and said, 'Bit early to go yet though – come into the Chateaubriand restaurant and have a bite of lunch'.

What a Cup Final day I had – one of the best seats in the house and no work to worry about.

4

GRADUATION

It is the flagship of BBC Sports Department's fleet, it is another hell or heaven, it is terrifying to anticipate, and fantastic when it is over. I speak, of course, of *Grandstand*, which has been the burden of my Saturdays for ten years or more. For the whole of Friday, when normal, sane human beings are looking forward with relish to the end of a good working week, and savouring that 'Friday night feeling' – the anticipation of an exciting weekend of leisure ahead – I am not at all nice to know. I am abrupt with the family, preoccupied in the company of friends. The immediate prospect is terrifying: five hours without a script, not really knowing, despite every precaution, what's going to happen next, with a cacophony of voices in your right ear every minute of the way. Yet, when *Grandstand* works well, when the team is in full professional cry, and the sport is good, it can be the most marvellous five hours.

In the late sixties David Coleman was the presenter. He'd made his considerable reputation from being able not only to take talkback in his ear, change his mind in a trice, get his facts right, and most of all, sight-read the football results on the teleprinter, but also to interpret and amplify them in the most amazing way. Coleman was the only one who could tell you that that win had put Arsenal on top of division one on goal average, or that that was East Fife's first score draw in nineteen consecutive games. He still is. Nobody does the teleprinter (or the vidiprinter as it now is) like him.

He had presented the programme for ten years, from the autumn of 1958 when it began. Peter Dimmock, the man I'd followed into *Sportsview*, had tackled the first two programmes, after which Coleman came to London from the Midlands to take over. By 1968 he felt he wanted to get out more, to shake off the yellow pallor brought on by the lights of Studio E, Lime Grove.

Graduation

Nest and I and the boys were in darkest Shropshire visiting my mother. She had no phone, but somehow an emissary reached us with a note in a cleft stick telling me to ring Bryan Cowgill in London. Clutching a fistful of pennies (do you remember, a phone call cost four old pennies in the sixties?) I went to the nearest callbox and finally got through to the boss.

'Where the bloody hell are you?' he demanded. He knew full well where I was, but the gentle approach was never a prominent feature of his man-management portfolio.

'Obviously Shropshire' I replied.

'Oh, never mind all that. Got a few things to sort out before the weekend.' I knew he was due to go on holiday in a few days. 'Listen', he continued. 'Want you to do a few more *Grandstand*s for me.'

At the time, I was presenting the odd *Grandstand* programme, though nothing very prestigious, mind. No Grand Nationals, Cup Finals, boat races or rugby internationals for me. Usually I got one or two of what we call the 'dog days' of the sporting year: the Saturdays in November and December when the light goes by 4pm so there is no possibility of live outside broadcasts, there is not too much sport about anyway, and we had dear Eddie Waring and little else.

Consequently I really was delighted by Bryan's request. *Grandstand* was *the* programme to do, and the prospect of covering some of the more important events was very pleasing indeed.

'That's terrific, Bryan' I said, enthusiastically, 'marvellous – er – how many?'

His reply I'll never forget. It slayed me.

'About forty-four' he said, emphatically.

After I'd expressed my delight there was one other exchange I remember before we hung up. 'We must also talk about money, Bryan', I said. 'Money!' he howled. 'What do you mean, talk about money', and he went off into a blaze of rhetoric, which lasted a full minute without him drawing breath. Bryan was so passionate about *Grandstand*, which he'd invented, as he'd always remind you, along with Sunday cricket and the slow motion replay, that I'm sure he felt you should be paying him for the privilege of presenting the programme. It was almost as though he was offering me the Holy Grail!

Thus I came to a very important crossroads. *Grandstand*

was to affect my life very considerably indeed. It is a great programme to do, and I've been identified with it ever since, but it hasn't all been good, particularly in the way the family have been affected. Every Saturday, virtually, was sealed off. In those days of the late sixties and early seventies I was still doing Sunday cricket, and indeed for eighteen months *Sportsview* as well, which meant none of the joys of weekend family life. Our three sons, David, Stephen, and now Andrew, have grown up playing football, rugby and hockey, and I've seen them in action hardly a handful of times, which is very sad. Organising a weekend away together, or even at home, is very difficult.

After my conversation with Bryan, we reorganised. I was to do 'about forty-four' *Grandstand*s while Coleman kept the very best sixteen. If you're adding up, by the way, and wondering how on earth there can be sixty Saturdays in a year, don't forget that Boxing Day, Good Friday, Easter Monday and all the Bank Holidays as well are *Grandstand* days. It really does add up to sixty a year, give or take one or two.

So instead of 'playing at it' from time to time, I was now totally involved. Before very long it became clear to me why the programme is such a success. First of all, you have got to have the events that viewers want to watch; that goes almost without saying. But that's not all. The way those events are presented has put *Grandstand* head and shoulders above any other sports programme in the world.

I am a salesman. It is my job to persuade you to watch my programmes, *Grandstand* and *Nationwide,* and not the opposition's. To do that one has to have a good product, and the BBC certainly has a good product. If you want to watch Wimbledon, the Test matches, the Boat Race, the rugby union internationals, the Gillette Cup final, the rugby league cup final, and have the Olympic Games covered thoroughly and at length, then you've got to watch *Grandstand*, because nobody else has all these events or spends the air time necessary to do them justice. Also, in order to have a programme that is reputable and responsible, you need coverage of great depth. BBC Television in 1979, for example, covered fifty-four sports – and even that isn't enough for some people. But that is a healthy sign. Fans want their particular passion on all the time. We never have enough racing for some people; others can't stand it, and complain that the horse is God, that we go too early to the paddock before the race, and stay endlessly waiting for the starting prices after it. But if you accept that it is a betting sport, you've got to cover it properly – and punters do want to see the horses, hear expert comment about their form, know the odds before placing their bets, and, of course, they want to know after the race how much they have won, if they have won. So *Grandstand* takes the sport seriously and provides the service the racing fans want.

At the other end of those fifty-four sports are the ones that are on the periphery of people's interest – in the grey area where we know there is an audience, but it is not a very large one. Could it be increased? Can we encourage interest in the sport? *Grandstand* and the sports department as a whole has certainly done that with sports like show jumping, which is now immensely popular with viewers. Until Foxhunter and Nice Fella and Sunsalve came along, most people were quite unaware of the sport. Similarly, snooker and darts are both much more popular now as a result of television exposure and presentation.

There are other sports that are simply difficult, if not impossible, to cover properly. 'Do you not know' people are constantly saying to me 'that more people participate in coarse fishing than any other active sport?' That may well be true, but what do we do? Set up a highly expensive outside broadcast team on a river bank and wait for hours until somebody gets a bite? Even if the anglers were pulling them out every minute, would people at home who are not anglers watch, anyway?

There are spectator sports and there are participation sports. For example, not a great many people can be persuaded to watch hockey on the box – they're all playing it, those who love it. It is essentially a participation sport. We do show hockey on *Grandstand,* and the indoor variety that has come along recently has helped to make it more viewable, but there will never be much of it. Similarly squash: 'the fastest growing sport in Britain', I'm constantly being reminded. That may well be so, too, but there's one small snag – on a television screen you can hardly see the ball. We've tried everything, white balls, yellow balls, and every conceivable alternative. You do have a chance if Mohibullah Khan is playing a delicate touch game, but if Geoff Hunt is belting the living daylights out of that tiny black object it disappears almost completely. Again, there will be some squash, but never a great amount. But never mind, fifty-four sports is a great spread of activity. We're always looking for more that we can cover, too.

Why do I think the presentation is so important? After all, the Cup Final is the Cup Final: that's what you've switched on to see, so why don't we just slap it on and forget it? I suggest you'd soon notice if we did. One of the nicest compliments anybody can pay me, and it's a compliment to the whole programme, is to say, 'Hey – what a great life you've got – five hours every Saturday afternoon. What the hell do you do for the rest of the week?' Well, you bridle at that a bit, because you think to yourself, don't they know about the homework, the meticulous preparation, the problem of timing, of mixing the *Grandstand* programme so that it never droops in the middle, of making sure events do not clash. There are a million and one problems that need to be solved before the programme can begin to entertain anybody. But that is the point: it should look easy. It should look as though I have just rolled into the studio at 12.14pm, and one minute later five hours of golden television unfold like some magic carpet. So if anybody thinks it looks easy, that is entirely as it should be.

How is it done? Well, that's a book in itself. At the heart of the programme is teamwork. The right people doing the right job, caring about doing it well, and with a burning ambition that their contribution is not going to be the bit that's weak, that rocks the boat, that is seen to be flawed. Ginger Cowgill, who laid the foundations for the programme, used to say 'I don't associate with rubbish, lad'. He employed a pretty rough rule of thumb that sorted out the people who produced their all from the posers and dilettantes. His method was often painful, nearly always acrimonious, but it worked.

The programme's groundwork is laid way in advance when contracts are signed with the various sporting bodies. Some events, therefore, we can block into the programme months – even years – in advance. Rugby union internationals, the Cup Final, the Boat Race, Wimbledon, the big race meetings, the Test matches – they have all been negotiated and paid for so we know they're there.

For the management team on the programme, like the editor and the producer, the programme is a six-days-a-week job and often more if it is an Olympic Games year. My own involvement with the programme starts on Friday morning, when I join the production team to tackle in detail the following day's *Grandstand*. It is a day of plans and homework and checking and worrying. By Saturday the whole team has assembled. Three or more outside broadcast teams, each with its own producer/director, at places like Headingley for rugby league, Newbury for racing, and Crystal Palace for athletics, are locked into the mother-ship as it were, with mission control being Studio E, the *Grandstand* gallery in Lime Grove, Shepherd's Bush.

On the studio floor, several distinct groups are preparing to make their particular contribution. Tony Cornell, a top-class quality journalist if ever there was one (he's with the *Daily Mirror* during the week), is marshalling his sub-editors, Adrian Brown, Ron Wills and John Belliss. Together they will take in, assess and knock into shape all the sports news that comes in during the afternoon from all over the world – perhaps a Test match in India, or the running scores of a full football league Saturday afternoon. What Tony doesn't know about football and the people who play it could be written on the back of a torn Cup Final ticket.

At the other desk is John McCririck, our racing ace. He's a big, noisy fellow, but all he cares about is making sure that our racing operation runs like quicksilver – particularly our own televised meeting. From him stem betting, starting prices, results, in other words the whole works as far as racing is concerned. John is with *The Sporting Life* for the rest of the week, has a voice like a sergeant major, thinks racing should take precedence over other 'minor matters', like an Ian Botham 100 or a Coe world record, or even the end of the world. He is always offering information, and that's what he's there for. He and Harry Heymer, who is a long-serving stalwart of the programme, run the racing desk superbly.

Then there is John Tidy. You wouldn't know him. But if there's one man on the whole of the operation whose absence would show more than any other, it is John. The editor, the producer, Frank Bough – all are replaceable, but not John Tidy. He does all the graphics: the football results, the cricket scoreboards, the rugby union scores, and captions with the latest positions in this, that or the other event which we are going into or leaving. All the information has to be faultlessly correct, and produced with breathtaking speed in front of a camera to show the world. At least, graphics is what John and his team of checkers and craftsmen are paid for: but in the middle of a most demanding sequence of events, John can manage to find you a cigar, a cup of tea, or a pencil, and even a fact or two on the position in the drivers' formula one championship, or the christian name of an obscure American golfer. He's a magician, pure and simple.

The engineering team, meanwhile, are going through their paces. Vision lines have to be arranged from all sources, from a major outside broadcast to a one-minute report that is due in from the Nottingham studio on the Forest game, much later in the programme. Then there are sound lines, so that the commentator, and the crowd, can be heard from Newbury racecourse, and so that the said reporter in Nottingham can be heard when his moment comes, as well as seen. Finally, control lines are needed so that the *Grandstand* producer in Studio E can talk to the producers in their control vans at, for example, Newbury, Crystal Palace and at Headingley, Leeds. Everywhere the cameramen are checking their equipment, lining up shots, and framing the best pictures for your consumption.

In videotape another irreplaceable team of people, led by Campbell Ferguson, are checking their equipment, making certain their contribution to the day is beyond reproach. They are deciding on which videotape machine they are to record the racing, so that we can show a highlight at the end of the afternoon, and likewise with the athletics, should it be needed. When two events are going on together, they'll have to record one, so that we can show it to the audience after the first has finished. Are they on cue with the week's boxing package, recorded last Tuesday at the Royal Albert Hall? And have they got ready all the clips, a myriad of them, for Bob Wilson's *Football Focus*? As likely as not they will have been working into the small hours of Saturday morning, or even all night, selecting the pieces of action required at different times of the afternoon and editing them to the right length and in the right order.

That was the kind of *Grandstand* team, already well-honed, that I had the privilege of joining in late 1968. Around that time there were two other newcomers to the programme with key roles – a new editor and a new producer. The new editor was Alan Hart, the man I had met in Newcastle in the early 1960s on that hectic night when Sunderland were playing Manchester United in the Cup. I had worked for him before, too – he'd been editor of *Sportsview* for three years and also had done many of our *Review of the Year* programmes.

Graduation

Whereas Alan was immensely tall, the producer, Brian Venner, was a shorty – in fact he'd coxed the Oxford University boat crew in 1956. Cambridge won by a length and a quarter, but I bet Brian Venner harrassed them all the way. He was immensely energetic and from the time he'd joined the BBC the only job he'd ever wanted was producer, *Grandstand*, and now he'd got it, having survived Ginger Cowgill's ordeal by fire with flying colours. He was to become a producer of great talent.

So the three of us embarked on a journey of great exuberance, that was to last for ten years before Alan became Head of Sport and Brian left the Corporation to join another television organisation. We had to get used to each other's professional habits so that each of us knew what the others were most likely to do in an emergency. It became a very rewarding professional relationship, though often argumentative in a way that must seem curious to those outside the business. But when people care about something as much as the three of us cared about *Grandstand*, there are bound to be healthy arguments about the methods of achieving the very best results. Through the famous earpiece, of course, I could hear everything that passed between them.

'Shut up, Alan, you're distracting me.'

'No, I won't shut up, you're getting it wrong.'

'I know what I'm doing, Alan.'

'Who's running this bloody programme.'

'I am.'

'No, you're not, I am.'

'Shut up, Alan.'

'*You* shut up, Brian.'

I could only hear the words of course, but the visuals were hilarious. They sat alongside each other at the control panel in the gallery, with Brian looking up towards the ceiling where Alan's head seemed to be, and Alan peering down out of the stratosphere at the small man alongside him. All that mattered was the programme. We all cared so much, and stayed very firm friends despite the pressures of the day. In the bar afterwards all was forgiven and forgotten.

Grandstand was like a regular Saturday affair between the three of us professional bedfellows, working our socks off to present a glittering array of sporting events that is still the BBC's annual sporting calendar. And it was not just the Saturdays, either. There were the great television sporting marathons too – the Olympic Games, football World Cups, European athletics championships. We saw Tony Jacklin's hole in one, the first hole in one on television. We saw Brendan Foster win a great 5,000 metres European gold medal, and that delightful lady, Lilian Board, achieve her European athletics gold in Athens. She came into the studio when she got back to take part in our highlights programme. Everybody adored her; she was pretty, sexy, and bubbling over with all the joys of a life that was soon to be ended, tragically, by cancer.

One must not forget great Cup Finals, either, the presentation of which was meticulously planned by Alan and executed with great dash and professionalism by Brian. The relationship stood rock-steady through hours of Olympics events with hardly a moment after the end of the programmes in which to hammer out words and running orders before the next was upon us. Our professional habits were invaluable at moments of stress like that.

There were also some marvellously funny moments. For example, one of my annual nightmares is interviewing the winners of the rugby league cup final in the Wembley tunnel after the match. We would catch the players right at their joyful moment of victory, talk to them in the maelstrom of photographers and fans, show them their tries and good moments, and generally capture the thrill and atmosphere of the occasion. The trouble is that few rugby league players have instantly recognisable familiar faces, and however hard I study the formal team photographs of the finalists, they look completely different when they have just played a hectic cup final. Faces run with sweat, they are swollen, cut and bruised, hair is all over the place, and the players are almost invariably without their teeth which are wrapped in a tissue in the pockets of their suits hanging back in the dressing-room! On one occasion I was about to talk to the captain of Widnes when he said 'Hang on, Frank', and whistled down the tunnel for the trainer to bring up his teeth, because there was no way he was going to be seen back home being interviewed without his upper set firmly back in his mouth.

Apart from the problems of recognition, it is difficult getting the players you really have to talk to in the order you'd ideally like them because, perfectly understandably, they are all anxious to do another lap of honour round the stadium. The captain must be interviewed, as well as the try-scorers and the winner of the Lance Todd Trophy, awarded to the man of the match.

Well, I had done the captain and one of the try-scorers, and was looking frantically out of the corner of my eye for another hero who was nowhere within sight. Making time for myself, I threw a question to a man just behind me who for an instant I thought was a player. 'Do me a favour, Frank', he said, 'I'm the bloody coach driver!'

A host of unwittingly funny lines were produced by *Grandstand* commentators, too, looking for the right phrase in an emergency. For example, one of the problems of an Olympic Games is that there are twenty-one sports across the board, and inevitably amongst them are one or two that may be passionately followed in other countries (like, say, cycling is in France, Belgium and Holland), but which get little coverage on BBC Television because we can't persuade viewers to watch them here in any great numbers. Now we have a great breadth of commentary talent in the BBC, with specialist men in most places. Peter O'Sullevan – racing, Harry Carpenter – boxing, David Coleman and Ron Pickering – athletics, Peter Alliss – golf, Alan Weeks – ice skating, Bill McLaren – rugby union, John Motson and Barry Davies – football, Dorian Williams – equestrian events, and David Vine, who is an all-rounder. It is a very impressive list of commentators, who really know their sports inside out.

But, as I say, when it comes to an Olympic Games, somebody has to apply himself to a great deal of research and homework into sports like rowing, cycling, volleyball, and so on, which we do not regularly cover. The danger there is that having done all the homework, the commentator understandably likes to show off a bit. I was presenting the 1972 Olympic Games from Munich one day, and handed over to the rowing regatta course at Feldmocking. A few minutes later the commentator, in full flow, produced a real gem. As the competitors went past the thousand-metre mark, he remarked: 'You'll notice in this event they're carrying their cox in the bows.' Fifteen million viewers collapsed in hysterics!

Actually Feldmocking is one of those names which a presenter fears, in case he gets it the wrong way around. It is a very difficult word to get out, once you realise the implication if your teeth are not in straight! It is the same when Coles and Hunt are playing golf together: one slip, and you may as well pack up and go and work somewhere else. And you try saying in a hurry 'And now we're going over to Shitecova in the shot'. It has got to be right, hasn't it?

Incidentally, while I'm talking about the pitfalls that lie in wait for the unsuspecting commentator, I always thought the man who came closest to disaster was Alan Weeks during a commentary on the great Speedway Internationale at Wimbledon, one of the top events in that sports calendar. Now as you know, speedway is over very quickly. It really is noisy, too, as the exhausts roar, the cinders fly and the crowd goes mad, and the commentator has to bang away very loudly to be heard at all. Pool Alan. As the bikes thundered round, over the far side of the arena, he found himself shouting: 'And there he goes into the lead, fighting his bucking machine!' When I next saw him, I said 'My God, Alan, did you realise what you nearly said?' 'Yes', he said, 'as the words came out of my mouth, a great sweat broke upon my brow'.

These, of course, are the commentary lines that are born of over-enthusiasm for the British cause. That is one of the criticisms most often levelled at us when we're doing a big international event like the Olympic Games. It is said that we go overboard for the British competitors, that we are over-chauvinistic, over-jingoistic, have red, white and blue stripes before the eyes, wave the Union Jack too violently and bang the British drum too loudly. I don't think it is too bad a fault, but I do know what the critics mean.

For example, one day in Munich in 1972 I'd handed over to the canoe slalom course at Augsburg. The Germans, with their Teutonic efficiency, had created a wonderful man-made course of rocks and rapids for the event. After a while, there suddenly appeared on the screen the British kayak pair, upside down in the rapids, wedged very firmly against a rock. All you could see was the bottom of the boat. Our commentator chose that moment to say: 'I don't wish to appear pessimistic – but I sense our medal chances are slipping away.' Too right they were! Anyway, I thought that line deserved some kind of gold medal for exaggeration until a couple of days later it was far surpassed by an absolute peach at the swimming pool. At one point in the swimming programme there was a fairly lengthy race in progress. During it, a British competitor turned at one end almost half a length of the pool down on the current leader of the race. 'Well, quite clearly, at this stage in the race' said the commentator, referring to the British swimmer, 'he's content to let Mark

Graduation

Spitz make the pace'! You may recall that Mark Spitz won seven gold medals in the Munich Games . . .

The best clanger from a fan I ever heard reported was told to me by our engineer who was covering the concourse at Twickenham before a rugby union international between England and France. The French always bring their own distinctive flavour to a Twickenham game, in the way of national costume, barrels of red wine and loaves of French bread, and also cockerels. The cock is their standard, their symbol. The problem is they actually bring live birds just to prove the point, and many is the letter I've had from bird lovers deploring the fact that we've shown the poor creature on camera before and during the game. It appears on this occasion that a small knot of French supporters were making their gentle way through the crowds to their seats, complete with berets, Gauloises, the lot – including a cockerel hidden beneath a jacket, with its red crest and beak protruding over the lapel. Alongside them was a group of Londoners, ribbing the Frenchmen as they moved in together and making no bones about the fact that they were going to rub the collective French nose in the Twickenham turf that day. But apparently the message wasn't getting home. The French were inscrutable, clearly having no English. So one pursuing Cockney, determined that the French should understand, summoned up just about every schoolboy French word he had ever learned. His voice cut through the winter air. "Ere' he said. 'Cette apres-midi le lion anglais mangerai votre cock.'

But during the late sixties and seventies when I was presenting *Grandstand* with Alan Hart and Brian Venner, standing out above the weekly Saturday presentations were the marathons, particularly the Olympic Games. The actual competition at a Games lasts a fortnight and there is so much going on morning, noon and night that the programme scheduling on Olympic *Grandstand* was almost total. We were hardly ever off the air. A football World Cup competition actually lasts longer, spanning three weeks, but because the football matches are played at weekends and in the middle of the week, there is always an opportunity on the non-football days to have a break and draw breath: but not during an Olympic fortnight.

The whole effort reminds me of an event we used to have in the Victoria Baths swimming gala in Oswestry when I was a boy. It was called The Long Plunge. The competitors launched themselves into a dive at one end of the pool and had to allow their momentum to carry them as far as it would. No arm or leg movement was allowed and the head had to stay sub-merged! As each competitor either sank or blew up, the distance was measured. An Olympic Games was just like that for our BBC *Grandstand* team. We all plunged in one weekend and emerged exhausted and completely shot a fort-night later.

I'd been to the Tokyo Games in 1964 as a reporter/commen-tator, but the first real telly marathon I embarked upon as a presenter was the Games of 1968, which were held in Mexico, at an altitude of seven thousand five hundred feet. In prepara-tion for the thin air, competitors had spent time at altitude for months before, to give themselves a chance of matching those, like the Nigerians, who had been born and lived all their lives at that height.

Because of the time difference between Britain and Mexico, seven hours, it was decided that the daily Olympic *Grand-stand* programmes should be controlled and linked from London. That meant we could present the afternoon events in Mexico into the night London time, and thus record the evening competitions and hold them until Britain was awake again and able to watch. Hence, a murderous idea emerged, for a breakfast programme called *Good Morning, Mexico*.

The idea was this. Our main, live blockbusting *Grandstand* would start at 8pm on BBC-1. We would follow the events live, sometimes until two in the morning or beyond. We would be back on the air at 7am for a programme lasting two hours, which would show highlights of the Olympic evening events like boxing and basketball, which had come over the satellite in the preceding four or five hours. There was another programme after that at lunchtime, and yet another in the evening for viewers who had been at work all day and who had not yet caught up with the previous night's competition.

What a devastating schedule that was, for all concerned. I would link the evening programme until the middle of the night, and then catnap in my Television Centre dressing-room while other members of the team took in and edited new material. Then I would be up at six to prepare the *Good Morning, Mexico* programme from 7 to 9am. If you've ever had to be bright-eyed and bushy-tailed at that hour of the day, after being up until all hours the night before, and keep it up every day for weeks, you can imagine how I felt.

Graduation

I would then have breakfast at a local hotel, and at about 10.30am crawl into bed. The lunchtime programme was presented by David Vine, and then I'd be called at 4pm or so after five hours of daylight rest to do the evening highlights programme. No sooner was that over than another six-hour evening stint began at eight. Day in, day out – and night too – the work went on for a whole fortnight.

I began to find that I was at my best for the breakfast programme *(Good Morning, Mexico)*, bounding around full of vitality surrounded by ashen-faced colleagues, who had been up all night editing new coverage. Conversely at 8pm, when really I needed to be at my sharpest, I could hardly stay awake.

By the second week the pace was beginning to tell. There was such enthusiasm for the whole fortnight that people pushed themselves too far. One producer, sitting at the back of the control gallery, suddenly put his head in his hands and wept. He had given 110 per cent and had nothing left. Even the iron man himself, Ginger Cowgill – who was running the operation and driving himself beyond reason, grabbing a few moments rest when he could – finally caved in. He couldn't think any more, could hardly speak, and almost forcibly had to be propelled out of the action for a couple of days rest. Paul Fox, at that time Controller of BBC-1, took over the helm. I, meanwhile, lost a stone in weight and achieved the extraordinary feat of suffering jet-lag without actually going anywhere!

The problem of high altitude was taking its toll in Mexico too. In the distance events, oxygen was constantly being given to exhausted competitors. Ron Clarke, the great Australian runner who over the years had established eighteen world records, was reduced to a zombie in the 10,000 metres.

The Kenyans, though, flourished, accustomed as they were to being at altitude and with their lungs developed accordingly. Keino won the 1500 metres, Temu the 10,000 metres and Amoss Biwott, the steeplechase.

For Britain, it was a disappointing Games in the athletics stadium where it really counts. While world records fell thirty-three times in track-and-field, and new Olympic records became so commonplace that in the end, nobody bothered to count, only David Hemery achieved complete happiness. He destroyed the rest of the field in the 400 metres hurdles, winning by a street in a new world record time of

48.1 seconds. His was our only athletics gold medal.

A young Lilian Board, hot favourite for the 400 metres, came second. She was caught in the straight by an unknown French girl called Colette Besson.

Our horses did well as usual; and then we all had to wrap our tongues round *Supercalifragilisticexpialidocious,* as Rodney Pattison and his crew man, Iain MacDonald-Smith, brought her home to a gold medal in the Flying Dutchman class in the sailing regatta. Dick Fosbury of America ensured his immortality by launching himself over the high jump bar backwards. The Fosbury Flop was born.

News of *Superdocious,* I recall, reached us during the latter part of the second week five minutes before we were to go on the air with the 8pm evening *Grandstand.* We scraped the very barrel of our staying power, and in two minutes flat rewrote the whole of the opening part of the programme to accommodate the sailors' feat. We were so weary, I recall, that the rest of the six hours passed in a haze of exhaustion.

I do remember with pleasure, though, that with our body clocks turned upside down because of the crazy hours we worked, the one mooring-post of the day was a breakfast with Brian Venner each morning after the *Good Morning, Mexico* programme. We hung on grimly to that simple, daily habit as a moment or two's respite during a very stormy fortnight indeed.

But, you know, during the whole period (and I assure you it was wearing beyond belief), the *Grandstand* teamwork held wonderfully firm! As total exhaustion struck first this member of the team and then another, somebody was always at hand to plug the dyke. I don't believe there is a television company in the world that can match that depth of talent, or that total belief that the programme comes first, second and third, and after that what matters anyway.

Four years later, the Games came to Europe, to West Germany, to Munich. The demands on the devotion and skill of the sports department were much the same, except that after Mexico it was realised that too much had been asked. In 1972 the manning of the programmes was a little more generous; lessons had been learned about the importance of looking after body and soul a little better. How could we have guessed what additional demands were to be made at an Olympics which for two days, 5 and 6 September, turned into a nightmare.

Graduation

To start with, we were all in Munich. This time the Games were to be presented and linked from the site. The facilities for which we had to compete with the rest of the world were modest to say the least. *Grandstand* had a tiny studio – the *Maus Haus* we called it – with room for two cameras, Chris Lewis, the studio manager, who was to look after me, me and a small desk. I was to spend virtually the whole fortnight locked inside it, with Chris and his bumper book of old, awful jokes! They were to keep our spirits going through some depressing times, as the whole Olympic ideal was put to mockery.

There were, of course, some great moments, and some even greater personalities. Mary Peters, from Northern Ireland, won the pentathlon: her face, as she watched the computer scoreboard in a crowd of her fellow competitors, working out the points and the medal placings, ran the gamut of emotions from anxiety to hope and finally uncontrollable delight, as she learned she had won the gold medal.

The delightful Olga Korbut burst upon the Olympic stage with a display of ingenuous bravura in the gymnastics hall that charmed the whole world. It was extraordinary that she only appeared at the Games as a reserve competitor, when one of the Russian-selected girl gymnasts became ill and couldn't compete. There were wild, deeply emotional scenes as she won three gold medals, her waif-like figure floating through apparatus and floor exercises. Each ended with a delightful smile and a cheeky wave that became her hallmark. Valeri Borzov, her compatriot, became the fastest man in the world, the elegance and style of his sprinting matching Olga's performance. Dave Wottle of America, dubbed 'the head waiter' because of his habit of leaving his winning burst so late it was unbelievable, won the 800 metres, wearing throughout a ridiculous, tatty, even dirty, cap.

We shared, too, the agonies of David Bedford. The Munich Olympics were to have been his Games. His talent was undoubted – he had recently, at Portsmouth, run a dazzling 10,000 metres in the second fastest time ever. But his uncertainty, his self-doubts, camouflaged by a brash, boasting exterior, sank him in the end. After front running for lap after lap, his opponents stayed with him, and finally destroyed him.

At five o'clock on the morning of Tuesday, 5 September, a German television reporter left the Olympic television centre. As he passed the adjacent Olympic village, where the competitors lived, he thought he heard a shot. He only gave it a moment's thought, and went on home to bed. One hour later, he and dozens like him were aroused with the news that Arab terrorists were in the Olympic village, that one member of the Israeli team was dead, and a number of his colleagues were being held hostage.

The scene in the Israeli block was visible, just, to one television camera: the one perched at the top of the television communications tower, about half a mile away at the edge of the Olympic Stadium complex. The camera was turned round, away from the centre of Olympic competition, and zoomed in as far as it could go to hold a fixed shot that was transmitted to the whole world for one long, unreal day. The attention of Olympic Munich turned with it.

An ultimatum was thrown out by the terrorists. Release two hundred Arab political prisoners and guarantee us safe passage out of Germany, or the prisoners will be shot by 9am. David Coleman joined me in the *Maus Haus*. Accurate information was hard to come by. What little we did have was fed into David's ear, as first the nine o'clock deadline passed, then another at eleven, and then a third at midday.

The Games continued eerily. The world continued to run and throw, to swim, to play basketball, as the awful drama continued through the day. The agony of being compelled to say after every critical report, 'In the meantime we return to the basketball hall where the score at the moment is . . .' was quite the most difficult job I've ever undertaken. Yet the Games went on. Finally, at 3.30pm all competition was suspended. At 9.20pm we were on the air again as helicopters were heard overhead. Coleman, exhausted by now (he'd been on and off the air all day), was back again at 10pm. The tower camera still watched. Fox still fed Coleman with what scraps of news he had.

Eleven o'clock: a further report of shooting at the Fuerstenfeldbruch Air Base. 11.30pm: The German government issued an official statement to the effect that all was well. The hostages had been freed at the air base. Three terrorists had been killed, and the rest were being pursued.

The relief we all felt at the end of the day was enormous, in particular for the members of the Israeli team who were alive and safe, and for their broadcasting team who shared our television centre corridor. Coleman had done a superbly professional job too, backed by the rest of the team, under the most difficult circumstances. Sleep was blissful.

Breakfast on the following day, 6 September, came like a sickening blow to the stomach as the news appeared. The rescue the previous night had all gone horribly wrong. The news which had sent us to bed the previous night, so relieved, was wholly inaccurate. At the airport, police had opened fire on four of the terrorists as they approached the Boeing plane ready for their departure. Two had been killed and one wounded. From one of the helicopters carrying the hostages leapt another of the terrorists, who had thrown a grenade back into the aircraft as he left. In the other, the terrorists had opened fire on the hostages inside.

There were no survivors amongst the hostages. Later that morning in the stadium the Olympic movement, shaken and polluted by what had happened, gathered to remember the dead. A movement where brotherhood and goodwill and hope for mankind were held to be paramount, had been used on a public stage where hate and death had been paraded. The whole of Olympic Munich was laid low with a most terrible depression. The Games must stop. How could Olympic athletes go on playing and rejoicing after what had happened?

Israel, mourning her dead, was insistent. The Games must go on; anything else, and terrorism would be seen to have triumphed. Avery Brundage, eighty-four-year-old President of the International Olympic Committee, agreed. The Games must continue.

Certainly in the BBC team there was a growing conviction that despite the fact that the competitions were to be resumed, there was no way after the events of the past two days that we could present them in Britain in our usual way. There had to be some pause, some brief mark of respect. The feeling gained momentum, and almost became a demand that we should not transmit sport that night.

In the end we went on the air in the evening with a brief report that chronicled the events of the two previous, awful days; we showed the scenes at the memorial service held earlier, and tried to find the words to express how we felt. I closed thus: 'This evening, in the boxing hall and at the weight-lifting stadium, the Olympic Games resumed. The events cancelled last night took place tonight. The full programme of athletics and the rest starts up again tomorrow morning. It's our job to report them and we will – but not tonight: tomorrow morning.'

5

A GRANDSTAND WEEKEND

What follows below is a reconstruction of a weekend in the life of Grandstand, *to give you some idea of the complications of putting together the five hours of live television that I keep telling you about! The weekend I have chosen was an unusually difficult one, as you will see: the action takes place in Cardiff, Putney, the Television Centre, and Studio E, Lime Grove, London. The date of transmission is 17 March 1979 – but first there is the preparation . . .*

London: Thursday

Another March. Another Wales/England rugby union international. This year it is the turn of Wales to be the hosts, at that magnificent cathedral of a rugby ground at Cardiff Arms Park. The size of the occasion, the excitement of it, is for me anyway the equal of a Cup Final, a Lord's Test match, or a Grand National. The Arms Park, Murrayfield, Twickenham – all have their different atmospheres on an international Saturday, despite the fact that the game is the same. But Cardiff Arms Park has something extra. First, Twickenham and Murrayfield are in the suburbs of London and Edinburgh respectively, while the Arms Park is situated right in the heart of the Welsh capital city. It is the hub of Welsh life for several days; Welsh rugby union international weekends start about Thursday, and for many people don't finish until the following Monday. For rugby lovers, and Welshmen in particular, enjoying an international represents a big slice of the quality of life. Additionally, for the Welsh, rugby is the right arm of the national corporate body – along with their language and their music, it is part of their whole identity. They also play the game like demons and revel in success!

I must get the cuttings out, and familiarise myself with the whole picture. I don't need to check England's record in Cardiff. In ten years of presenting *Grandstand* and making the pilgrimage to the Principality every other year, I've never yet seen England win there. You have to go back to 1963 for that, sixteen long years. Could it be that this time, as well as enjoying the whole wonderful occasion, the hospitality, the comradeship, the faggots and peas parties, could it be that I will taste the real spice of an England victory in Wales? I say this before every match, but in 1979, after a long period of poor results and disappointments, England go to Cardiff with a highly prestigious victory under their belts. A fortnight ago they beat France at Twickenham, playing very well in the process, and their tails are up. Surely England have a great chance, since Wales have been decimated by the retirement of a whole clutch of their great players – Phil Bennett, Gerald Davies, Gareth Edwards, Terry Cobner – while for the mighty JPR Williams, this is to be his last game for Wales. On this March Saturday in 1979, England, Wales or France can win the International Championship. France are playing Scotland in Paris. We have a great programme in prospect, because Saturday is also Boat Race day. Harry Carpenter and I are co-presenting the programme, he from the river at Putney, me from Cardiff.

God, the weather's awful. Watch the Cheltenham Gold Cup on the office set. Tied Cottage, running a beautiful race in driving snow, leads all the way and falls at the last fence. What an unpredictable business sport is. I'm sure that the unexpected happens at least as often as the expected. That's why it is a fascinating pleasure I suppose. How do I travel to Cardiff on Friday? It is no weather for driving – the M4 will be hell. I'll take the train. Check times, get ticket organised. Tickets. All season I've promised Stephen, my second son, that I'll take him with me to a Wales/England game in Cardiff. He plays such a good game of rugby, at full-back for his school; has a good pair of swaying hips, and yet I've seen him play only half-a-dozen times, if that. Why haven't I seen him play more? Weekend family life has been non-existent for years due to *Grandstand*. Has the experience of doing a job that a million sports-mad people would love to do been worth the sacrifice? Sometimes I think not.

I ring Steve to check that he's still keen to come. Yes, of course, but he's got a hockey match at school. He wants his school hockey colours more than he wants to see Wales play England. That's good. I'm pleased at that. Must ring Dewi Griffiths in Cardiff, the Welsh producer who covers the game for us, to cancel arrangements for Stephen. He'll have no trouble getting rid of the ticket – all of Wales, and a large part of England, want to get into the ground.

It is bitterly cold. What to wear on Saturday? Boots, always boots on cold days, long johns, ski-socks, sweater ... *two* sweaters ... sheepskin. Hat? I always look ridiculous in a hat. I've tried several to keep the cold from entering the bald patch on the top of my head. No. I'll suffer bare-headed. Gloves. How many pairs have I lost? Note to call into Maidenhead and get yet another pair.

At least I warm to the prospect of the match. How am I to make every second of five and a half hours count? Find fresh words to describe a familiar scene at the Arms Park? Sweeping North Stand, huge crowd, passionately committed to the team and studiously well-behaved too. My in-camera position will be on the track near the halfway line, with the whole North Stand to my immediate left: twenty thousand people. It is like performing in front of the largest theatre audience in the world – never a beer can thrown, or an orange. Remarkable crowd behaviour.

Over the years they've watched me enjoy some rare moments too, as I've linked the programme for the hour or two before the match begins, talking to the pundits about the game to come, handing over here and there to the other sports in the programme, before we concentrate on the big game itself. It was there I first met Max Boyce. I'd been down to Nest's family in Wales, and they were full of this new Welsh balladeer singing about the great rugby occasions, capturing the characters and the partisanship, and making wonderfully funny observations about the Welshness of the occasion. I listened to his first LP – Max Boyce was a young ex-miner making his first steps in show business, and was relatively unknown then, even in Wales. It seemed to me a splendid idea to ask him along to my position there in front of the North Stand to hear his stories, freshly drawn, about Welsh rugby. When he did appear he was a delight, and the following week sent me a copy of that first LP. On it he'd written: 'Thanks, Frank – after the *Grandstand* bit I leapt to number four in the LP hit parade!' We've had him back several times since, and now of course he is well known throughout Britain.

On a later occasion in front of the North Stand, he presented me with a large, mounted, colour photograph of a symbolic coffin with himself lying on top draped in the Welsh flag, being buried at sea by his musicians. 'You see, Frank. I've had this terrible dream.' And there in the corner of the photograph was a mythical final International Championship table. At the top, it read 'England played 4, won 4, 8 points'. At the bottom, 'Wales played 4, lost 4, no points'! The chances of that ever coming true are extremely remote!

There was also Precious McKenzie, Great Britain's diminutive weightlifter. He, too, joined me under the great North Stand, not for a Wales v England game, but for Wales v New Zealand. Precious, whose skills won so many honours for him and his country, had moved to New Zealand and now lives there. He had come back on a visit and there he was at Cardiff, this time supporting the All Blacks from his adopted country. In front of the camera we talked about his new life and he gave me the badge showing a little sprig of fern, the Kiwis' emblem. 'You're looking well, Frank' he said, and suddenly, with everybody looking on, *I* was being interviewed by *him*. I had recently worked off some excess weight, and was a bit pleased with myself. 'Yes, Precious', I said. 'I was getting a bit large so I had to do something about it. I'm now the weight I was when I was eighteen. I reckon you'd have no trouble with me now.' I meant that as a light remark, certainly not as an invitation. But Precious took it as such, and in a trice I was whisked up in the little man's arms like a baby, microphone and all. 'I'm losing control of this programme . . .' I cried. It can be quite entertaining down beside that pitch!

However, this time, as well as hoping for the odd unexpected event that is so much a part of live television, I wondered if England could actually win the big game.

Friday
Today I'm due to travel to Cardiff after lunch for the international tomorrow. Friday is a day of great anxiety for the *Grandstand* production team. I join the editor, New Zealander Harold Anderson, who's been in the chair for just over a year; Martin Hopkins, the producer, who directs the cameras in Studio E in Lime Grove, and coordinates all the material on the programme – be it a live visit to a 2.30 race at Newbury, the running of last Tuesday's big fight at Wembley which will be on videotape, or a telejector slide of a footballer who has scored a goal. It is Martin's job to ensure that what the editor wants to do, at any time of the afternoon, happens. It sounds

easy put like that, but an immense amount of planning is needed to achieve the smooth running of the programme. That is particularly true of this weekend, with me a long way away in Cardiff, hearing them all the time through what we call 'the deaf aid' in my ear; Harry Carpenter will be down on the river, similarly attached, and so there are two highly prestigious sporting events to be coordinated. The Boat Race is an especially complicated outside broadcast with fourteen cameras spread down the course and one in a helicopter high above it.

The three of us – editor, producer and presenter – meet in the editor's office at 10.30 plus Alastair Scott, another of our producers, who is going to direct my linking camera in Cardiff. With us are some of the people who make it all possible, the assistant producers and production assistants who work in the videotape area in the Television Centre (and that is also a mile away from the control room at Lime Grove). Videotape is so much a part of the television scene; if we didn't have the best operators in the business as we do on *Grandstand,* the programme couldn't exist. Harry Carpenter is with us too.

There are two big problems looming ahead. One is the weather, which is still lousy. There's nothing we can do about that, but if the Chepstow Saturday race meeting is off (and there's a chance it will be, with a Friday inspection that afternoon at 3pm), we'll have to rearrange our planned running order and find some extra sport in a hurry to fill the time taken by three National Hunt races.

The other problem is one of timing. The Boat Race start time changes each year with the varying time of the flood tide, and this year it is perilously close to the kick-off time at Cardiff. The Boat Race is at 2pm, the Arms Park match at 2.30. If the Boat Race has a late start – crews have been known to get up to a bit of gamesmanship at the stake boats to ensure it does – or it is a slow race, or there is a sinking, and we've had two of those on *Grandstand,* we could miss the kick-off in Cardiff. Also the singing just beforehand: that's unthinkable. We go through the ifs and buts, trying to anticipate all the various permutations that could be forced upon us by weather or timings. After that, we can only light a few candles and say a few prayers.

I ring Dewi Griffiths in Cardiff to arrange to meet him at the Cardiff Athletic Club, the home of Cardiff Rugby Club, and on international weekends, Welsh rugby. He and I also need to talk about our roles on the big afternoon, and make sure each knows what the other is doing. Gradually the jigsaw is being put together.

Nest rings from home with a great piece of news. Stephen has been made a senior prefect at his school, Desborough, a comprehensive in Maidenhead, one of the very best. That really gives me a big extra kick. It is a large school, and has a big sixth form which he's only just joined. His new status is a real honour, bestowed by the head boy and senior prefects. I do my proud father bit, and tell everybody in sight.

Noon – it's still snowing. I drive home and assemble my programme kit ready for a trip to the Arctic. Nest drives me to Reading to catch the Cardiff train. One of the advantages of the train, apart from letting British Rail take the strain, is that I can get some homework done during the journey. But such hopes are dashed – the train arrives crowded – standing room only, everywhere, and I'm jammed upright between the lavatory and the luggage rack for the whole journey. Blast!

For *aficionados* and fans alike, Cardiff Athletic Club is the forum in which on a Friday evening the morrow's conflict is dissected and analysed, and where after the match on Saturday the victors (almost invariably the Welsh) toast their success and commiserate with the losing visitors. The place is packed. There is a commissionaire on the front door, but I've never known anybody, reasonably dressed, not to be admitted. Everybody, it seems, is due to meet somebody and will only be five minutes.

On this Friday, like every other, the Welsh are indulging in their familiar exercise of brainwashing the visitors. The method is to adopt the attitude of no-hopers.

'Well, boys – with the big five gone – what hope do we have? '*Duw* –your boys played well against the Froggies – play like that tomorrow and we're dead.' 'We're so bloody makeshift at the moment.' I know the patter so well, and my usual response is derision, but this time, fingers crossed and trying to convince myself that by the very law of averages, we've *got* to beat the Welsh in Cardiff sometime soon, I agree with them. Lead with my chin.

'We'll have you tomorrow. Team's in great form. I've seen them lose here so often but tomorrow – you're right – we're going to beat you.'

This nonplusses them somewhat, since they're used to being

reassured that however bleak the Welsh prospects, fire and spirit and individual brilliance will conquer all. It usually does. The Welsh are classic manic depressives. One minute you're hanging on to their coat-tails as they take off into an ecstasy of exuberance and enthusiasm, the next minute you're digging them out of the slough of despond and urging them to stop moping and get the hell on with life! In rugby, as in many aspects of their natural inheritance, they're concerned as much with *how* they do things as how successful they are.

I once had the great privilege of attending the international team dinner after the match, at the Angel Hotel. (Across the street from the Arms Park of course, so the *hwyl* lingers on!) Wales had just beaten the French to win the Grand Slam – played 4, won 4 – which meant that they'd achieved the mythical Triple Crown as well, having beaten England, Ireland and Scotland. So their season had been monumentally successful. However, they'd spent the last half hour of the game grimly defending the Welsh line against a series of French attacks, of the sort in which they specialise. Improvisation, running, swift, clean handling, the French can go mad like nobody else, and it's a frightening sight for the opposition. But the Welsh had held out and victory was theirs. Nevertheless, the manner of it was not to their liking, 'all that defence, boyo'.

One of the Welsh forwards asked me at the dinner, 'How do you think we played?' worry all over his face.

'My God' I replied. 'You ask me, an Englishman, how I think you played. You've won everything in sight and England today have lost at home to the Irish to register a whitewash. Played 4, lost 4' (shades of Max Boyce's dream!) 'and you dare ask me how you played. Does it matter at this moment how you played?'

It did; it mattered to him desperately. Victory for the Welsh comes in two varieties. The matches you win and those you also win but as a result of brilliant, free-running, attacking, virtuoso rugby. That day, they'd only won, and it just wasn't good enough. He had sloped off, long-faced.

In the Athletics Club it is getting very noisy as the beer begins to bite, and old friends and heroes are greeted ever more enthusiastically. South Wales is rather like a largish village. Oh, there are the individual valleys with their allegiance to Aberavon, Bridgend, Llanelli, Pontypridd: there are other towns, other places, where the rivalry is intense, even bitter. But tonight, Wales is united against the army from over the Severn Bridge. Bleddyn Williams, Onllwyn Brace, Cliff Morgan, all are hailed. They are older, balder, plump with success, all ex-players now, but part of the Principality's folklore. To walk down Queen Street, Cardiff, with Morgan is to spend a lot of time doing it. He is greeted by strangers as an old friend, and hailed by bus drivers, who abandon their schedules for the chance of a few words with the old maestro. 'I remember Cliff, when . . . ' 'I was at the Arms Park, Cliff, when you and Bleddyn . . .' Oh to have given as much pleasure as those rugby heroes! I envy them that, as much as I wish I could have written Elgar's Violin Concerto. To have done either would have ensured me a happy death.

We English are received warmly, with the most immense hospitality. Alastair Scott, a Scotsman, trying not to look as though he has ended up at the wrong party, starts to enjoy his first Welsh rugby weekend. It's impossible not to. Bill Hardiman wends his way through the crush to say hello. I'm sure Bill has a title of some sort – groundsman, Arms Park stadium manager – who knows, but there's no tag to describe accurately a man who is part of the fabric of the whole place. He runs his empire with the most enormous efficiency and good nature from a small office, alongside the tunnel from which the players emerge into that great arena. It is full of rugby balls, autographed programmes, whitewash, rugby gear of every description, and his own private loo which has been my salvation several times during the heat of a *Grandstand* transmission from the Arms Park.

I was once asked by the *Daily Mail,* in collaboration with the cigar importers of Great Britain, to nominate for an award somebody who wasn't necessarily in the public eye, but who I thought had made an especially significant contribution to the sport with which he was associated. I looked no further than Bill Hardiman, and he came up to London for the presentation lunch wearing a suit. I hardly recognised him, since I'd never seen him wear anything other than the track suit that is his Arms Park uniform. In a very swish West End private club, Bill stood up and made the prettiest speech you could imagine. He was the hit of the occasion. What an ambassador for his country and for Welsh rugby in particular.

On one visit to an international Bill asked me if, after I'd handed over to Bill McLaren for the match commentary, I'd like to watch the game from the bench. It was a tremendous thrill to sit on the touchline with the game thundering to and fro across my eyeline. So close, and from that angle, the pace and power of the game of rugby is breathtaking. And pounding at your back is that great volume of sound from the huge crowd in the North Stand. Ever since, he's kept a corner for me on his own little row inside the rails by the players' tunnel, and it's from there I'll watch the match tomorrow.

Apart from the sheer pleasure of being in the Athletics Club on the Friday evening, it is of enormous help to me to join in the talk, hear the arguments, with the Welsh lilts growing ever more prominent as the time passes. Tomorrow, what Mervyn Davies said to Gareth Edwards about the composition and morale of the Welsh pack might come in very handy indeed. Time to go, though, before the graph of pleasure rises too high. A quiet dinner and sleep are the next two most important events in my calendar. The path to the door is strewn with more greetings, including Bryan Cowgill's cousin down from Clitheroe for the match. Must have a pee before we go. Ah, blessed relief. 'Hello, Frank' from the next head. 'Funny thing, life', said the man. 'Last time I met you we were having a pee together at Ninian Park when Howard Winstone was fighting. 1965 I think it was. How have you been, then?'

Saturday

A Welsh dawn, and it's dry, thank God, over the Park Hotel. In the few hours before a *Grandstand* programme all the little things have got to be right. This morning they're not. The hotel has failed to come up with all the papers I wanted, particularly the *Western Mail,* which on match days tends to ignore minor issues like the economic future of civilisation and the Russian nuclear threat, and instead provides an excellent ten-page picture and comment supplement on the only thing that does matter, i.e. Wales's match with England. I've also left my 'deaf aid' in London – and run out of cigars. Not a good start.

Harold Anderson is on the phone from London, anxious about the weather. Chepstow is off, but fortunately the snow has stopped somewhere on the border. He is relieved that the match is not snow- or ice-bound. The rest we can safely leave to Bill Hardiman.

On the telephone we go over the opening of the programme again. This is the only part of *Grandstand* that I actually write down, and then memorise. It is the laying out of our stall, describing where we are that day, what the issues are. It is a contents bill, and with broad strokes we lay our sporting day before the viewers. Facts to check: should be Wales's fourth, not third, consecutive Triple Crown – if they win, that is. Martin Hopkins and the videotape wizards have cut pictures to illustrate my words. Three words to every second of picture: it has to fit as tightly as that. He has the videotape pictures, of rugby, Boat Race, water-skiing, boxing and whatever else we have to talk about, running simultaneously on two videotape machines, and will wipe from one to the other as I talk. It's a straightforward exercise in professional television, and if the opening of the programme works well it puts us all in a good mood and sets the pace for the rest of the afternoon. With control exercised in London, we in Cardiff, and Harry chipping in with a Boat Race scene-set from the river, we're really testing the system today. Communications are everything. If we can all hear each other clearly we'll be all right. What a twit I am, forgetting my 'deaf aid'. I have a personally moulded one, to fit comfortably in my right ear. I'll have to borrow one from somewhere, it'll be somebody else's and won't fit. Something else to do, an unnerving, stupid interruption to the smooth run-up to the programme.

The opening words I have still to write. I like to do them as late as I can, so they're as fresh and up-to-date as possible. After the scene-sets, we busk it. Create the links, the in-vision words between one sport and another as we go along. *Grandstand* doesn't use autocue, the prompting system where the words appear in the camera lens. Time is flying. I'm due at the ground for rehearsal at 11am, the programme starts at 12.15. I can't quite find the words I want. How do I make the most of what should be a tremendous occasion, and yet with economy of language, too? No waffle, but crisp, informative prose. The trouble with television sport is that we're constantly rabbiting on about 'great occasions', 'historic races', 'classic confrontations', so that when you really need an honest superlative to describe something that truly *is* great, the superlative is devalued.

I haven't found time yet for breakfast, and don't look like doing so. That's stupid. It's going to be a long, hungry day. By the time I reach the ground I know I'll have no appetite for anything. The stomach twists, with concentration and apprehension I suppose. Not with worry, that's different, but apprehension, the fear that I won't make enough of, or

possibly not recognise, every opportunity that a live programme presents, and which pass my nose every second. I've
prized a copy of the *Western Mail* from the Park porter, make
myself a cup of coffee from the do-it-yourself kettle, munch
the chocolate biscuit. What is JBG Thomas saying about the
match this morning?

In the middle of it all, a call from the *Sunday Mirror*. How
the hell have they found me? Television gossip. They've heard
David Coleman is presenting the Cup Final for the BBC this
year: what do I have to say? (It's too long a story. They'll only
write it up as a row anyway.) 'No comment'.

Now I'm feeling thoroughly wrong. Too relaxed, too confident, too irritable, I don't know how to describe it, but I'm not
sparked up enough. I've got the opening words on eight-by-
five cards. I hammer out the very first words I'm to speak, and
pace the small room talking out loud, pouring the phrases and
the facts into my memory. I do this all the time, even in
public. I like to hear how they sound. One day two men in
white coats will come and lead me gently away!

Check. Cards in right order. Pass to get into ground. Match
programme. *Western Mail*. Notes. Programme running order.
Deaf aid. Blast! What *am* I going to do for a deaf aid? Two
Pentel ball pens. Clip board. I'll be working in the open, no
protection from the elements, no sophisticated comforts.
Everything has to be at hand, in its place. I am properly and
warmly dressed.

A ten-minute walk from hotel to ground, through the centre
of Cardiff. Streets already teeming with groups of excited
Welshmen. Red and white everywhere. Wasn't there a tobac-
conist down here somewhere? I go a block too far and have to
go back. Stick two packs of Villiger Export in overcoat pocket.
There's my deaf aid! Things are looking up.

Once at the ground I go to my linking camera position near
the entrance to the players' tunnel. The new North Stand,
empty now, rears away steeply to my left. Behind me, it
curves round to the posts as it meets the River Taff, which
flows past the end of the ground. It is a Welsh outside
broadcast unit that's covering both the linking of *Grandstand*
before and after the match, and the game itself. The cameraman, who is to point at me, hidden, muffled behind his
viewfinder, and the sound engineer with us, are both likely to
be as excited as anyone later today. Greetings all round.

The sound man gives me the two thin cables that will

enable me to function for the five-and-a-half hours the programme lasts. One is a microphone: clip to tie. The other has a small round disc on it, to which I attach my personal deaf aid. It fits snugly into my right ear, plastic lead going over and behind the ear, all out of view.

I now have in my ear, and will have for the rest of the day – until the match has been won and lost, and the programme completed at 5.20 – the combined voices of all those in the control room of Studio E, Lime Grove, London. Mission control with a vengeance! Editor Harold Anderson will be relaying decisions to me, to the wizards in videotape down the road in the Television Centre, to floor manager Charles Balchin, who's alongside me in Cardiff, and graphics king John Tidy on the floor of Studio E, and to Martin Hopkins, the producer, who will use the same channel of communication to make it all happen, and direct the cameras accordingly. I will hear the vision engineer worrying about the quality of incoming rehearsal pictures from the Boat Race cameras; the sound engineer, checking his multitude of lines to and from wherever sound is needed; the engineering manager, coordinating all the complicated technical requirements that bring a picture to your screen; and Penny Wood, the producer's assistant, keeping a remorseless check on timings, second by second. I can hear them all, and need to know and listen to the problems being discussed so that I can be ready to paper over the cracks if need be. At any given moment, they can hear me when I speak into my microphone, whether I'm off or on air.

In the Welsh control van, parked under the great North Stand nearby, is Alastair Scott. He has control of the Arms Park cameras before the match, so that he can direct the interviews I do before the game begins, and show the crowds gathering and all the accompanying scenes. He will hand over to Dewi Griffiths just before 3pm, and Dewi, using the same five cameras, will cover the actual international. At the press of a switch, Alastair can override all the talkback from Studio E, London, and talk down my ear as well, so that together we can arrange any sequences, his pictures matching my words and *vice versa*, as the atmosphere intensifies during the early part of the afternoon. I say good morning to all, and to Harry Carpenter on the tideway at Putney. Yes, Harry and I can hear each other too!

Think about it. It's a crazy way of making a living.

In the midst of all the chatter – with every member of the

team, editorial, production, engineering, each intent on his own business, each beavering away to ensure that when the programme starts, his part of the whole will be working perfectly – I exchange cues with Martin. Every time a piece of videotape is run, and there will be dozens before the day is spent, Martin needs a word cue from me to know when to run the videotape machine. It takes ten seconds for the pulses in the magnetic tape to lock into a picture, so on each word cue Martin howls 'Run VT' and each time Penny Wood will count down from nine to zero. During that time my words have to fit precisely, at the rate of three words to every second. If I don't fill the gap, I stand there with egg on my face, because Martin can't cut to the pictures at the precise moment we're aiming for until the ten seconds are up, and if I overrun the ten seconds, I'm chopped off in full flight. It is as precise as that, and it is the television presenter's nightmare.

In the opening sequence, we have several tape runs in rapid succession. Taking each introductory link, I count back thirty words, and give the word to Martin, who writes each down carefully. If I forget to utter the word, or he misses hearing it, we're in trouble. I underline every word cue at my end, just in case. *(These vital words are printed in heavy black type in the reconstruction of the programme which follows, so that you can spot them easily.)*

We stagger through a rehearsal of the opening, with frequent stoppages to deal with points as they arise. We've decided on a pre-title start – that is, both Harry and I appear in rapid succession before the *Grandstand* opening music and picture appears. Then it's me, at Cardiff, setting the scene for the main issue of the day – a Championship table cut in from London, showing the current positions before the last day of matches today. Then it's me, leading to a compilation on videotape of great moments in the career of JPR Williams, the Welsh captain, playing his last match. Then it's me again, then the Championship table again, to make the point that England can also win the title, then a videotape compilation of the best of England's play during the season. Then the table for a third time to illustrate the part the French, playing Scotland in Paris, can play. French action next. Then me again, with information on the time of kick-offs, what we plan to do, which match we can see where and when, and a word about the weather.

Then I'm to hand to Harry at Putney, who gives the same

set-up treatment to the Boat Race. Back to me again. Explain how the racing at Chepstow is off, and then run a piece of videotape of the basketball, our other sport that afternoon, a national championship semi-final we've recorded earlier in the week between Doncaster and Coventry at Wembley. Me again, giving other sport, mostly football matches that have been destroyed by the lousy weather. Then hand to Bob Wilson for *Football Focus*, because it's League Cup final day. Nottingham Forest are playing Southampton at Wembley.

The whole opening sequence is just eight minutes long. Eight minutes out of three hundred and fifty minutes of programme, the only eight minutes we can rehearse. We try it again and again, and a third time, honing and polishing until all the parts are running smoothly. Throughout, we have a sound problem. The talkback, from everybody to me, is crystal clear one minute, then there's a click, and it is as if they've all gone to the moon. I can hardly hear them even with the big stadium empty and quiet. If the fault persists during the programme when the crowd is in, it's going to be hell. As things turned out, it did, and it was!

It's ten to twelve, twenty-five minutes before transmission. I'm pacing up and down the touchline, with my second cigar of the morning, muttering the words, trying to carve them into my memory. Bill Hardiman appears, cheerful as ever. He's heard there are blizzards everywhere, except in Cardiff, and he's prepared a peach of a pitch on which he's convinced Wales are going to thrash England yet again. He has kept me a seat at the front of the stand, on his staff bench. Don't forget, the loo is there should I need it. I do. I disentangle from my wires, dart down the tunnel and turn left into Bill's little kingdom. Somebody's pinched the plastic lavatory seat. My God, the china rim is cold!

Five minutes to the off. I'm back in front of the camera, plugged in to all systems again, and ready. As ready, that is, as I'll ever be. This is the moment every Saturday when I'd happily be anywhere else except where I am. In the pub, weeding the garden, watching the boys play football. All the lovely, sane, ordinary things that sensible human beings do on Saturday.

'One minute to transmission' – Penny Wood. Thank goodness she's in my ear. The very best there is. They all are. What am I fretting about? 'Good luck, Frank, Harry, everybody' from Harold and Martin. Likewise. 'Stand by Cardiff.'

Cue Frank!

'Cue Frank.'

CARDIFF

LONDON
STUDIO E, LIME GROVE

Frank
'Today, *Grandstand*'s big spring double. Here at Cardiff Arms Park, Wales versus England on the last and decisive day of the rugby union International Championship.'

'Cue Harry'

Harry
'And here on the River Thames at Putney, Oxford and Cambridge fight out the Boat Race.'

*'Run titles . . .
9-8-7-6-5-4-3-2-1-go!'*

We're off! Titles are on the air, they're playing my music again. Concentrate. Whip through the next few words to be sure.

'Cue Frank'

Frank
'What a finish to the rugby union International Championship. Here at Cardiff Wales play England, and in Paris, France play Scotland, and at the end of the day any one of the three of them could end up as champions. Wales certainly could. They head the table. *(Somebody's taken the championship caption off the stand and not put it back. Hell!)* Victory over England would mean that they'd keep their title *(relief!)*, and win their fourth successive Triple Crown as well. They are led today by the great **JPR**

'Helen, where's the bloody Championship Table? Get it in!'
(That's Martin, to Helen Wienhold, our floor manager in Studio E.)

'We've got it! There it is, Frank'

'Back to Frank'

Williams playing his 52nd and last game for his country. And how often this fine player has kept his best try scoring efforts for the English.'

'Run VT . . .
9-8-7-6-5-4-3-2-1-go!'

'On VT for 54' (that's Penny)
'Championship table next'
(Martin) 'And don't move it,
Helen!'

I breathe for 54 seconds, silently curse whoever dislodged the championship table from its stand, mutter the next words, and check where we're going to next.

'10 seconds left'

'Cue Frank'

Frank
'So Wales are the favourites but England can also win the Championship. The first requirement is that they **beat Wales** here in Cardiff, a tall order since they haven't won here since 1963 but England this season have shown the form that suggests that victory is at least possible.'

'Cut to table'
'Stand by VT'

'Run VT . . .
9-8-7-6-5-4-3-2-1-go!'

'On VT for 42'
'Championship table next'
'10 seconds left on VT'
'Cue Frank'

In the middle of all this, while England's form is being displayed, there's a click in my ear, and they all disappear to the moon. Sound engineers are pulling and tugging at wire connections all around me, still trying to locate this infuriating fault. There's another click and they're back in my ear full strength.

Frank

'But England's championship hopes also depend on what happens in Paris, where a **French** victory over Scotland could give France a chance of the title. And the Scots no doubt saw how inventive and dangerous the French can be in their game against England a fortnight ago.'

'Cut to Championship table'
'Stand by VT'

'Run VT . . .
9-8-7-6-5-4-3-2-1-'

'40 on VT'
'10 seconds left'

Frank

'So Wales, France and England all with championship hopes. The Paris game kicks off at two, so we'll know the result of that one before the end of the game here in Cardiff, and we'll have highlights of it after we've seen Wales against England. This one kicks off at 2.30.'

'Cue Frank'
'We're on you Frank'

'Weather next' (Harold)
'On your shots, Ally'
(Martin to Alistair Scott)

'We've been hearing a few minutes ago from Jack Scott about blizzards in the north, so in this lousy winter we're lucky to have a cloudy but dry day here in Cardiff. It's cold, but nevertheless, the pitch is a beauty.'

'Putney next'
'Stand by Putney'
'Stand by Harry'

'Well the weather often plays a significant role in the other half of our great spring double and that's the Boat Race. What's it like on the River Thames, Harry?'

'Cue Harry'

A Grandstand Weekend

Harry's due to do a couple of minutes from Putney, building up the Boat Race, so I have a moment or two to marshal my thoughts, to see if sound have found the reason for the break-up of my talkback. It's okay now, but they don't know yet why it's coming and going. Hell, I can't live through the day like this.

'Wrap it, Harry'
'Stand by Cardiff'
'Coming to Frank'
'Cue Frank'
'Stand by basketball VT'

Frank
'As to our other sports today, we've no racing, the meeting at Chepstow has been **snowed** off – like many other race meetings in Britain today. But as well as the Boat Race and the England/Wales rugby international, we've *Football Focus* in just a moment and basketball, one of the semi-finals of the National Championship between Doncaster and Coventry at Wembley. The basketball is at 5 to 1.'

'Run VT . . .
9-8-7-6-5-4-3-2-1-go to it'

'Cue Frank'
'Stand by Bob Wilson'

Frank
'By the way, racing's not the only sport to be hit by the weather today. There are 26 football matches off, 24 of them on the coupon, and we'll give you the complete list in a moment. So what a day in prospect. I'm at Cardiff, Harry's on the river, and Bob Wilson's going to Wembley for the League Cup final between Nottingham Forest and Southampton. Here he is with *Football Focus*.'

'Cut to Bob and cue'

Cue Frank!

For me, the opening fury of the programme has subsided. I have twenty minutes or so during *Football Focus* to gather my wits, and work on my next link, my next interview. (There are two coming up, one with David Duckham, the England midfield star, who has just announced his retirement, the other with Gareth Edwards, who is now with our commentary team, talking about JPR on the day of *his* final appearance.)

I feel I have survived the opening minutes, but just to get by is never enough. We're not in the business of just getting by on this programme. Was my delivery clear enough, emphatic enough? The viewer only hears the words and sees the pictures once. Was the planning right, was the execution crisp and sure?

In any case, the opening of *Grandstand* is the barometer by which we set the standard of performance for the afternoon, and the morale of everybody in the team. If it goes well we're away, up to thirty thousand feet in a twinkling, and flying smoothly. If it's weak, if there's a mistake, then we can waste another hour or so, building ourselves up to the peak we had hoped to climb in those few vital opening seconds, but didn't. It was all right today. All right. But all right's not enough. Did it show that that damned caption was late on the screen? Did the anxiety show in my eyes or was it hidden? Did I hesitate? Stumble? When the sound in my ear disappeared into the far distance, my heart leapt I know. Did it show, did it show? Underlines my anxiety this morning to be in exactly the right frame of mind, with the right mixture of relaxation and concentration.

That is by no means unique to my business. Grand prix racing drivers, footballers, cricketers, all sportsmen, rejoice in that marvellous feeling when they're in form, whatever they're doing. Their mental and physical sharpness is clean-edged, and their confidence is full. In my business it is never more manifest than in the way I cope with talkback. To speak confidently and lucidly to camera, while still managing to take in a direction in your right ear, can be a most elusive talent. Somewhere in the well of my concentration, a shutter, a centre-board has to divide the bit that's coping with what I'm doing from the bit that's taking in the voices of others, the instructions and changes of plan. Sometimes the partition is perfectly made. There are days I feel I can do almost anything, cope smoothly with any eventuality, perform all sorts of mental gymnastics. That's when the shutter is perfectly

Left: Aged five, at 10 Tirley Street, Fenton, Stoke-on-Trent – my first home. We lived here until I was six, and then moved to Oswestry in Shropshire.

Below: The wild bunch? No, just the head boy surrounded by his prefects at Oswestry Boys High School.

Above left: A subaltern in the 2nd Royal Tank Regiment, 1956.

Above right: A happy day at St Mary and Oswald's Catholic Church, Oswestry, on 25 July, 1959.

Below: Army days in Munster with Chris Bonnington, the mountaineer (on my right). Note his pre-beard look!

Above: The day I arrived in London – in June 1964 – with Peter Dimmock. (BBC)

Below: Linking the 1968 Mexico Olympic Games from London – or how to suffer from jet-lag without leaving Shepherd's Bush! (BBC)

Above: An interview with Graham Hill, after the horrific crash at Watkins Glen in 1969 in which he nearly lost his life. (BBC)

Below: Chatting to one of cricket's legends, Frank Woolley, as we watch a Sunday game at Maidstone in May, 1969. (Kent Messenger)

placed. Other times I stumble along, unable to deal adequately with either what I am saying to camera or with the requirements demanded of that part of my brain just behind the 'deaf aid' in my right ear. Today was all right. Life's like that. Mostly all right, but imperfect.

At the moment though, getting the shutter in the right place is Bob Wilson's problem. I can hear it all going on. Bob's in Studio E, Lime Grove, and Harold and Martin have turned their full attention to him. Countdown to videotape clips of goals, some lasting only a few seconds. Talkovers, film, camera cues, telejector slides of famous players in the news. Changes in his script, as the football scene changes, as the game nears its regular Saturday afternoon three o'clock orgasm.

Bob has taken to television so well, applying himself to its professional habits and disciplines as methodically as he did to his goalkeeping. He is remembered in the game as a 'built' goalie, meaning he had limited agility and athleticism, but a keen, intelligent mind which he applied to the science of goalkeeping: the study of angles, of perfect positioning, of the strengths and weaknesses of his constant enemies, opposing centre-forwards. He had something else though. An immense courage, not to be found in coaching manuals, which often launched him to the thundering feet of opposing strikers. Bob's approach to television has been along the same thoughtful, professional line that made him such a fine goalkeeper.

Bob dines out on the story of how I quite unwittingly floored him on the day he did his very first match report in the *Grandstand* Final Score sequence. It was his first day on the programme, and believe me, putting together a minute report on a match is as difficult as anything he's had to do since. Belting back from the game, trying to sort out the facts and a few opinions, to be delivered off the top of your head in perhaps, forty-five seconds, to a minute maximum, is a nightmare for a new boy. He called for, and was given, a variety of advice. David Coleman cut through all the cotton wool. 'Look' he said, 'don't worry so much. Your football knowledge is immense and that will carry you through – no problem. But, on the way back from the match, make certain you sort out the first line you're going to deliver and hammer it into your head. After that it'll all flow naturally – but get that first line right.'

Bob's report was to be on his own club, Arsenal, who that

day were playing Manchester United at Highbury. Alan Ball scored after twenty-five seconds and then again later in the match to give Arsenal a 2-0 victory. Bob had his opening line, which he repeated and repeated to himself, over and over again, in the car rushing him back to the studio. 'I've just got back from Highbury, where Arsenal beat Manchester United by two goals to nil and Alan Ball was the star of the match.' Again and again he hammered it into his memory. He rushed into the studio, just in time for me to introduce him.

I turned to him and said 'Here's Bob Wilson, who's just come back from Highbury where Arsenal beat Manchester United by two goals to nil, and it seems Alan Ball was the star of the match – that right, Bob?' Collapse of Wilson – open-mouthed!

'Frank, on the phone'

It's Harold. I have another direct line to him, apart from talkback, for use when I'm not actually on the air, for the passage of extra information and news. At my feet on the cinders surrounding the pitch is an army field telephone, one of those with a little winding handle. In this computerised electronic age, the finest broadcasting system in the world still has in use an instrument of communication that likely as not was used in the trenches in World War I. It's even painted camouflage green!

(Harold. With information.) 'Newsreader will be Peter Woods and will you give out that the unseeded Sue Barker has beaten top seed Chris Evert 6-3, 6-1 in the quarter-final of a 150,000-dollar tournament in America and now plays Virginia Wade in the semi-finals; and that at Port of Spain, Trinidad, Australia are 204 for 7 in the first innings at the end of the first day of the World Series super-test against West Indies, and that Bruce Laird

> *scored an unbeaten 110 and*
> *that for West Indies Michael*
> *Holding took 5 for 36'*

Have you ever tried to absorb facts and figures like that in a few seconds, in the open air, with a telephone receiver held to your ear, a biro in the other hand, wishing you had a third hand with which to steady the paper? Last item of *Football Focus.*

> *'Stand by Cardiff – get*
> *in-vision Frank'*

Frank slams down telephone, stands on talkback wire, which unplugs, frantically replugs, stands in front of camera, and tries to remember 204 for 7, 110, and 5 for 36, and who they belong to.

> *'Coming to Cardiff. Cue*
> *Frank'*

Frank
'Thank you, Bob. He's now off
to Wembley for the League
Cup final and will be
reporting to us during the
match and at half and
full-time. Time for the news
from Peter Woods.'

During the two-minute news transmission, Harold's on the field telephone again.

> *'There's a row over the*
> *postponed Stoke/Sunderland*
> *football game. Sunderland*
> *turned back when they hit*
> *snow in Sheffield. Alan*
> *Durban, the Stoke manager,*
> *is furious because Victoria*
> *Road ground is perfectly*
> *playable and he can't find a*
> *football league official to*

Cue Frank!

complain to because they're
all at Wembley for the League
Cup final'
'Last news story' (Penny)
'Stand by Frank'
'Cue Frank'

The mental gymnastics required to take in a string of facts and figures at speed, and transmit them seconds later, totally accurately and looking pleasant with it, is the reason why currently my hair has just time to turn grey before it actually falls out. It's a close race, I can tell you. As I go through the Sue Barker victory, and the World Series Test score, and the Stoke/Sunderland/Durban details, Martin Hopkins in Studio E is going through his hoop too. John Tidy, the graphics king, has actually managed to put together a visual score-card of the Test score, Helen has produced slides of Sue Barker, Chris Evert, Virginia Wade, Bruce Laird and Michael Holding. While I'm on the edge of my concentration, making sense of the stories, Martin's poised on the abyss of his as well, listening to every unscripted word I say, punching up pictures as I speak to illustrate what I'm saying. The support for the presenter, the determination to maintain *Grandstand's* reputation for swift, accurate reaction to news is total. The teamwork is terrific. As the sequence nears its end, and I'm telling the Stoke/Sunderland story, part of my mind is thinking about what's next. But that's taken care of too.

(Martin)
'Basketball next. Stand by
VT'

Frank
'Now to the semi-final stage of the Rotary Watches National Championships at Wembley. In the first semi-final, Crystal Palace beat London Meteors by 100 points to 78. In the second, the one we're going to see, Doncaster and Coventry were neck and neck **throughout** and it was 29-all at half-time.

'Run VT
... 9-8-7-6-5-4-3-2-1--go to it'

We join it near the end,
Doncaster are leading 64-60
and playing in white.
Commentators are Miles
Aiken and Stuart Storey.'

Fifteen minutes of basketball, after which there's the David Duckham interview and then I'm due to lead to Harry for the Boat Race. Where's Duckham? Hasn't been seen yet. We're chasing. I look through my notes, memorising the points I want to make with one of England's most exciting players ever, on the day he retires. Several videotape illustrations. I pass the cue word for each of them to Martin in London. He makes a careful note. I'm aware that the gates of the Arms Park are now open. To my left in the North Stand, and all round the ground, the beginnings of a vast crowd are slowly assembling for the big game. Bill Hardiman passes the edge of my vision from time to time. It's his big day too. He's putting the finishing touches to his canvas, making sure his contribution to the day is without blemish.

David Duckham appears. Greetings. I explain to him the general form of the interview. About three minutes duration. Time slides by. I decide I'll run a piece of videotape Duckham action before actually revealing that he's alongside me. Tell Martin.

'One minute on VT'
'Stand by Cardiff – coming out. Cue Frank'

Frank
'Today here at the Arms Park
in the match to decide the
1979 rugby International
Championship, JPR Williams
plays his last game for Wales
against England. We'll pay
our tribute to JPR later. Also
today a famous English
international **announced**
his retirement from the
game. David Duckham,
without doubt England's
most exciting midfield back
since the war. Here he is,

'Run VT
. . . 9-8-7-6-5-4-3-2-1-go to it'

scoring a try in the match
against Wales in 1970.'

'30 seconds on VT'
'Give me Duckham, Cardiff.
Close up of Duckham.
Coming out, stand by, Frank.
Cue Frank'

Frank
'David Duckham is with me
here in Cardiff . . . '

David Duckham reflects on his great career, his famous partnership with John Spencer, his move from the centre to the wing, where he spent too much time waiting for the ball that never came, so that his superb running and swerving skills were neglected. Times don't change too much for England, and he wonders whether England's two wingers today, Peter Squires and Mike Slemen, both fine players, will fare any better. Wonders about the Welsh and their kidology; about JPR; about England's chances. Videotape is counted in my ear to illustrate the points we've planned. Picture matching words, point following point, as we plotted at the Friday meeting yesterday.

'9-8-7 . . .'
'About another minute,
Frank'
'Make this the last question,
Frank.'
'Don't forget the final clip of
Duckham action, Frank.
Stand by VT'

Frank
'David, thank you very much
for dropping by – and for all
the pleasure you have given   *'Run VT . . .*
to rugby followers all over the   *9-8-7-6-5-4-3-2-1 . . .'*
world. And finally here's
another reminder of the way
David Duckham played his
rugby.'

A Grandstand Weekend

Thank you David Duckham. Thank you for a decade of endeavour, of hard work, dedication and pleasure, in three minutes flat! David Duckham disappears, and we set the scene again for the big game. I look around and describe what I can see. Alastair flips in his overriding talkback from the control van under the stand, and directs the Arms Park cameras. The great sweep of the new stand, now filling rapidly as kick-off approaches. The state of the pitch, the weather. I keep an eye on the television monitor alongside the camera so that I make sense of the shots that Ally is selecting.

> *'That's the Country Club,*
> *Frank' (Ally)*

The Country Club stands at one end of the Arms Park ground, but outside the ground at a point where the terracing is low, so the Country Club balcony overlooks wall, terrace and the playing pitch itself. For years on a match day that balcony was packed to suffocation, as the members enjoyed a free view of games that the whole of Wales wanted to attend. Sad to say, the terrace is about to be rebuilt at a much higher level so the members' view will be blocked. The club has actually entered a plea that a hole be left in any new construction at that end of the ground, so that a tradition of decades might not disappear. It's a good Welsh story and I tell it. I state the position, the prize at stake. 'Wales can win the championship today, so can England . . .' If this, if that.

> *'Wrap it, Frank. Hand to*
> *Harry at Putney'*

Frank
'Now to the very different
atmosphere of the River
Thames in London on Boat
Race day. Harry Carpenter is
waiting.'

It's not time for the Boat Race proper yet, but there's the toss when the two university presidents meet to decide who is to select which side of the river, and there's an interview with the two young men as well. They'll be back to me in a few minutes time for the appreciation of JPR Williams.

Cue Frank!

I can hear Harry picking his way as neatly as ever through the minefield that is the Boat Race. As well as presenting the Boat Race in vision, he's also responsible for the commentary on the race. Normally on Boat Race day I'd be presenting *Grandstand* from the towpath, allowing Harry to concentrate on the commentary, but since today the England/Wales International and the Boat Race coincide, he's there and I'm here, which means Harry has additional problems. His talkback is giving trouble today rather like mine, judging from the complaints I've been hearing from time to time.

Harry is a real pro's pro. Immensely versatile, both in his knowledge of sports like boxing, which of course is his speciality, tennis, and golf, and his television technique. He's equally at home both commentating and presenting.

I'm reminded that one Cup Final day, when I was presenting *Grandstand* from Wembley, I was about to run a videotape recording of the week's boxing bill at Wembley when there was a local power cut in the Wembley area. The programme had to be picked up by Tim Gudgin, who was standing by for such an emergency in Studio E, Lime Grove. Tim rarely, if ever, appears in vision. He's a radio man, and reads out of vision racing results for *Grandstand.* When his big moment came he inadvertently ended his link to Harry's boxing by saying: ' . . . and the carpenter is Harry commentator'! Clive James, *The Observer* television critic, who must have been dozing at the time, thought it was me, and had a real howl at my expense in his column the next day. However, he was gracious enough to put the matter right the following week, ending up by saying 'I apologise, dammit!' Nevertheless, every time I hand to Harry either live or on videotape I go pale at the thought of saying 'the carpenter is Harry commentator'. The trouble is, now it's in my mind I'm certain that one day it'll come out.

Sadly, because Harry is so often somewhere else for the programme, we rarely meet, so it is one of my annual pleasures to co-present the *Sports Review of the Year* programme with him in early December.

At Putney, Harry is doing his usual impeccable job. At Cardiff, Gareth Edwards appears alongside me. Now here's a real superstar, and a delightful man. I'm privileged to have seen him in action so often, orchestrating the Welsh side from behind the scrum, marvellous in defence, pinching yards here and there with little runs, and those amazingly accurate kicks to touch. And in attack, what power. Give him a ball fifteen yards from an opponent's line, and he's through like a lance, carrying sixteen-stone forwards with him all the way, all hanging on to the little man like limpets but powerless to stop his forward impetus. He is to talk about JPR Williams.

Frank

'We'll be back at Putney before long for the Boat Race itself. Mervyn Davies, Barry John, Gerald Davies, Gareth Edwards, Phil Bennett – whatever our nationality we have to agree we've lived through an incredibly golden era of **Welsh rugby**. All those great names have now gone and only one of that talented Gallic clan remains. And today he retires as well. JPR Williams calls it a day and won't we miss him?'

'Wrap it, Harry. Stand by Cardiff. Cue Frank. Stand by VT – JPR Williams action'

*'Run VT
. . . 9-8-7-6-5-4-3-2-1 . . .'*

'One minute 10 seconds on VT'
'Coming out – stand by, Cardiff. Cue Frank'

Gareth Edwards is a delight to interview – give him a nudge and that soft, lilting Welsh voice talks about the game he loves and which he graced for so long. He talks of JPR's strength, his courage, and his skills. About the match – appreciative, he is, about England's recent form. Can't write them off, but you feel deep down that even without Davies, Johns, Bennett and himself he cannot conceive of Wales being beaten in Cardiff by England. Discusses his new career as a commentator. Interesting. He talks of the need to acquire new, professional, good habits for broadcasting. Being the best is in his blood. He knows that unless you work at something, the end product is always unsatisfactory.

'Make this the last question, Frank. Stand by Putney. Lead to Harry, Frank'

Cue Frank!

Frank

'Thank you, Gareth. We'll be
back here at the Arms Park
in good time to hear the
singing *(that's if the Boat*   *'Stand by Putney'*
Race gets off in time!) and for
the kick-off, but now we
concentrate on the 1979 Boat
Race between Oxford and
Cambridge. Harry.'   *'Cue Harry'*

The Boat Race is a big to-do. With so many cameras, it is a
television jigsaw puzzle. Radio pictures come from a helicopter, radio pictures come from a launch following the race, and
then there is radio sound as well. When it works it's smashing
– and it invariably does, thanks to the wizardry of BBC
engineers, in whose hands our reputations all lie. Will it be a
good race though? Last year we had a sinking, with great
excitement, but Oxford win early this year and it is another
procession. At least they got off on time, and our biggest
worry is over – the two events won't overlap.

At Cardiff in the Arms Park it's pandemonium. The place is
now full to bursting. The huge North Stand, curling round to
embrace the terrace at the Taff end, is a solid mass of heads;
the balcony of the Country Club looks in danger of collapse.
Also they're beginning to sing. No wonder the visitors here
are intimidated before they ever show themselves. As the
chorus filters its way down through every crack and crevice to
the England dressing-room, how does Bill Beaumont, the
England captain, persuade his team that they really are in
with a chance? I'm already beginning to regret my chauvinistic bravado in the Athletic Club last night. After all, I'm going
back there tonight after the match!

But suddenly – what a place to be, what a way to earn a
living!

'Cue Frank'

I can barely hear the scream from Studio E. *Calon Lân* is
rolling in waves down the stands to my left, cascading like a
Snowdonia tributary and forming a great river of sound with
the other stream that gushes from the stand on the opposite
side of the pitch.

A Grandstand Weekend

'Cue Frank!'

What words do you use, anyway? What vocabulary is there, instantly to describe the mood and the ferocity of this occasion. That lovely wordsmith, James Cameron, would have had a go, but reflectively, afterwards. The commentator's art is to conjure phrases out of thin air, to string them together as rapidly as the magician who pulls endless yards of little multi-coloured flags from the back of his hand.

'Cue Frank!'

Alastair is playing his buttons in the control van like a concert pianist. Sweeping wide angles, enveloping fifty thousand Welshmen. Close-ups of square dark Welsh heads, veins throbbing with vocal effort. The band master has abandoned his instrumentalists, left them to their own devices, and turned to conduct the stadium itself, his baton carving extravagant arcs through the crisp air as he strains to control the largest choir in the world. Who *needs* words, anyway? Turn up the volume on the sound desk and let it ride.

'Cue Frank!'

My talkback is still on the blink. I'm aware of instructions, but who knows what they are. The Arms Park reaches the end of a chorus. The sound fades as the crowd shapes up to the next hymn. Who decides what it is to be? Who decides the key? Who starts? Who knows! I take my opportunity.

Frank
'Below the stands the two
teams are now ready. In a
moment they'll be out to play
the deciding match in this
season's International
Championship – your match
commentator is Bill
McLaren.'

Carpenter, Coleman, O'Sullevan, Waring, Alliss, Williams, Gubba, Weeks, Motson, Davies, Laker, Benaud, Pickering, Wilson, West, Vine – the BBC's breadth and depth of commentary skill is well graced by Bill McLaren. He is the gentlest of men, who could have been a Scottish international himself had not an attack of TB nearly killed him as a young man, after he'd been a Scottish triallist. He was regarded as a certainty to make the Scottish side. His knowledge of the game is so highly regarded that after he'd seen France play South Africa, the Scottish team who were next due to play France invited Bill to tell them all he knew about the opponents' tactics.

After his illness, Bill never played rugby again, but now attacks the game of golf with the thoroughness and care that characterises all his work, be it teaching PE, rugby and Scottish country dancing to the children of the Scottish borders where he lives, or commentating on an international. Commentators are easy meat for the critics, but rarely have I heard a word of censure on Bill. He manages to accommodate the game's experts (and I've heard it said by internationals who have played in a particular game that McLaren got it virtually all right), and the youngsters who view the complex game of rugby for the first time. That's a rare talent. His wife, Betty, his two daughters, Linda and Janie, are all nuts about the game. Although he has no son, he overcame that problem by collecting Alan Lawson, the Scottish international, as a son-in-law, so a wonderful family unit is complete. On match days, he's also very generous with a particular Scottish boiled sweet, 'black bullets' he calls them, to 'wet the commentator's whistle' as he says.

Bill is now adding his immense authority to the occasion, which any minute now is about to explode with the appearance of the teams on to the pitch. The roar always starts at a precise point in the stand opposite the tunnel, where no doubt, one man is first to see the players deep in the well. As they approach the mouth and are visible to increasing numbers, the sound rumbles and swells sideways in both directions, until the whole stadium is bellowing its welcome. First appear the white shirts of England, led by Billy, prancing, leaping, exercising, passing. Anything to take their minds off the intimidating pressure of fifty thousand Welshmen, all enemies. Then come the Welsh, shirts deep red, the most coveted strip in Welsh sport. The roar intensifies, swells to a different note, welcoming, encouraging, totally supportive. It is a mighty moment.

The St Alban band strikes up the anthems. Two of them:

A Grandstand Weekend

God Save The Queen first. There are whistles and jeers from some, the Nationalists, but the mass of the crowd, knowing that Wales is on public view to millions of television viewers, sings with full throat. Good manners from a nation aware of its image. Then it is the turn of the Welsh anthem. From God knows where, the crowd moves into a fifth vocal gear. The whole fabric of the stadium throbs.

> *Mae hen wlad fy nhadau yn annwyl i mi*
> *Gwlad beirdd a chantorion enwogion o fri*
> *Eu gwrol rhyfelwr gwlad garwyr tramâd*
> *Tros ryddid collasant eu gwa'd*
>
> *Gwlad, Gwlad. Pleidiol wyf i'm gwlad*
> *Tra môr yn fur i'r bur hoff bau*
> *O bydded i'r hen iaeth barhau*

The Welsh XV stand in a tight scarlet circle, facing each other, bodies upright, heads high, each player singing his heart out, eye fixed upon eye diametrically opposite across the ring. Fifteen young men joining with fifty thousand fellow countrymen in common unity. It is without doubt an act of national communion.

With Bill firmly in the driving seat it's now time to remove myself from the touchline. In happier days when the BBC had money, we used to erect a small studio at the end of the stand at all the rugby international grounds, and this was the time I would go to it. It was warm, had a heater, a desk on which to write, a teleprinter line so that I was fed a constant and accurate diet of news and information, and a secretary to knock it into readable shape. In other words, all the support that a presenter has a professional right to expect, in order to accomplish his job properly. Alas, inflation and a niggardly licence fee (tell me what else you can buy in this life for nine pence a day?) has done away with all that. The temporary studio, including the facilities, used to cost £5,000 a time to erect and that was years ago. Money like that no longer exists. Do we also abandon the tradition of linking from the big events, too? Do we hell! The same performance is demanded of the presenter, in conditions that in any other industry would mean an automatic walk-out. I have linked the next two hours of a *Grandstand,* sitting amongst the band – several times.

Despite Bill Hardiman's hospitality, the present arrangement is no better. I return to his front row of the north terrace. I now have to watch the match from amongst the crowd, keep a close record of the scoring, recognise the tactics, the ebb and flow of the game, so that during the aftermath, I can ask intelligent questions of the two captains and the heroes of the day. Agreed, I do have a small monitor to help me, but since I'm on one side of the ground and our cameras are on the other, the play I can see on a level with my eyes is moving from left to right, at the same time the play on the monitor is moving the other way, from right to left! At various times during the match, while I'm trying to concentrate, I'm offered an orange, a shot of whisky, asked for autographs, and would I please move over so this bloke can go for a pee.

On the pitch, the game is even, but England are struggling to find the form that beat the French two weeks ago. Chances are missed, but not by the Welsh. Gareth Davies, the Cardiff scrum-half, drops a goal: Wales 3, England 0. Dewi Richards, the Swansea centre, goes over for a try: 7-0. Bill Beaumont is whipping up the English pack, but where is the control, the dominance, the unity? Away on the wind somewhere, blown by the Welsh chorale, which has started to lift the Welshmen towards victory. A penalty – Neil Bennett (of London Welsh; do we have to rely on them to score our points too?) thumps it over: 7-3. Are England coming back?

Throughout, on an only slightly rejuvenated field telephone, I'm trying to grasp the details of the Paris match. Harold is doing his best, hollering down the control line in Studio E.

> *'Latest score, Paris. Scotland 13 France 10. Sorry, France have just gone ahead – a Malquier try. It's France leading now 14-13. Scotland have come back. Andy Irvine try, 17-14 to Scotland. Conversion attempt hit the post. Malquier again, 18-17 to France'*

I'm trying to keep up, phone in one hand, biro in the other, jostled from left and right as the crowd swells and subsides with the action.

A Grandstand Weekend

*'And don't forget to hand to
Bob Wilson for a half-time
report on the League Cup
final at Wembley. You'll be
out of vision of course'*

The half-time whistle blows, with the score still 7-3 to Wales.
I try and assemble my brain while Bill McLaren and Gareth
Edwards summarise the events of the first forty minutes.

*'Stop talking Bill McLaren.
Cue Frank'*

As I sit forward on my seat, concentrating hard on the facts of
the matter in Paris and deciphering them as best I can,
sixteen Welshmen caught short by the excitement of it all and
their booze intake before and during the match, barge past me
towards the nearest loo. Half of them think the English must
be mad, since here's one of them talking to himself; two offer
me a drink; and one asks me how the Scots are doing in Paris.

Bob Wilson comes and goes. I hand back to Bill for the
second half. England are showing more spirit and the score
stands at 7-3, until JPR Williams, in a great clash of bodies, is
left lying on the pitch with a gashed leg. Hurried consulta-
tion, doctor on the pitch. The hero is led off. The acclamation,
born of the knowledge that this could be the way a great
player is to end his career, lifts the North Stand roof two
inches. The game resumes, and minutes pass while on some
consulting couch below, the doctor decides that JPR cannot
return, and a substitute is allowable. Surely we can score
against fourteen Welshmen. Can we hell. England press and
press, fifteen, ten, five metres from the Welsh line. But fifty
thousand and fourteen Welshmen are in defence, and that's
too many to beat. England fade under the effort of it all.

The public address crackles. 'The substitute at full-back
will be Clive Griffiths, Llanelli.' A slight, unknown, young
man emerges from the tunnel to roars of welcome, and
proceeds to play full-back with style and courage, as if he's
been doing it all his life. My God, where *do* they find them.
The king is dead – long live the king!

Mike Roberts scores a try: 11-3. Then Paul Ringer a try:
15-3. Then JJ Williams: 21-3. Elgan Rees, a try: 27-3. England are buried. Can I duck out of my date at the Athletics
Club?

Cue Frank!

I struggle down the tunnel, wires trailing, to my final linking position of the day (in the promenade under the stand), to catch the players, talk to them, lead to highlights of the France/Scotland game, give the rest of the day's news, and close the programme. The Welsh are already there in force to watch the final humiliation of Bough, once more at Cardiff and on the losing end. It's almost as good a spectator sport as the match itself. They press at my back, anxious for a good view, boisterous but very good-humoured. I plug in to Studio E again. The talkback problem, despite heroic efforts by the engineers, is still not solved, and in my ear, Harold and Martin are waxing and waning like England's hopes. My mind is fighting to find the words to run the videotape. Outside, the match is ending – the Welsh are carried home on a wave of hysterical jubilation. Behind me the tunnel fills with mud-soaked, battered players. The defeated form a gauntlet of applause for their conquerors: English to the last.

> 'Wrap it up Bill McLaren.
> Coming to Frank.
> Cue Frank'

I can hardly hear myself speak, so loud is the noise of celebration.

Frank

'So Wales have done it again – we'll see in a moment	
highlights of the	'Stand by Wembley'
France/Scotland match which	
had a second half of	'Stand by, Bob'
extraordinary fluctuating	
fortunes. But first there's just	
15 minutes left for play in the	
League Cup final. Bob Wilson	'Cue Bob'
reports.'	
(Bob Wilson does report, but	
is inaudible to me in Cardiff.)	'Stand by Frank'
'So we've seen Wales in	'Cue Frank'
triumphant mood, defeating	
England yet again here at	
Cardiff Arms Park, by 27	

points to 3. Now let's find out
what happened in Paris with
highlights of the game
between France and
Scotland. At half-time the
score was 10-all and we're
joining the game in the
second half with Scotland
attempting a penalty after
Aguirre had been penalised
for dissent. The commentator
is Nigel Starmer-Smith.'

*'Run
VT . . . 9-8-7-6-5-4-3-2-1-
. . . go to it'*

'30 seconds left on highlights'
'Stand by Cardiff. Cue Frank'

I go through the championship table. Problem is, although
everybody at home can see it, I can't. My monitor set, hastily
rigged, has not had the right picture fed through to it, and as I
look down all I can see is myself looking down at the monitor!
Studio E twigs and the team goes into emergency gear.
Harold reads the table into my ear, and I repeat parrot
fashion what he says. With support like that, where else is
there to go?

'Hand to Tony Gubba, Frank'

I do, and Tony orchestrates the football news from London:
teleprinter, League Cup final, match reports, pools news,
classified results, League tables, other news, late kick-offs, all
the information that *Grandstand* viewers have come to accept
as standard. In Cardiff we're sweating on getting JPR Williams. Journalistic pride demands that I interview him about
the game on the day the curtain falls on his own career. He's
still in the bath, or on the treatment table.

*'Stand by Cardiff.
Cue Frank'*

Clips of action from both games are now required to end off
the day, particularly for those viewers who have been elsewhere all afternoon.

Frank

'At Cardiff, Wales have done
it again, another
Championship, another
Triple Crown, their fourth in
a row, and all at the expense
of England, who they've
beaten 27-3 today. Here are
all the Welsh points.'

*'Run
VT . . . 9-8-7-6-5-4-3-2-1.
Go to it'*

We're still trying to winkle out JPR, to our cameras. Let's
have Gareth standing by to fill in just in case. These are the
drills, good professional habits, the bedrock of a good *Grandstand* programme. So many unexpected events today, so many
cracks in those carefully-laid plans of Friday, but all have
been papered over smoothly despite the difficulties – and on
air the programme has looked as clean and sharp as a new
pin.

'10 seconds left'
*'Stand by Cardiff.
Cue Frank'*

Frank

'And in Paris, in the other
game played today, a great
see-saw match saw France
beating Scotland by 21 points
to 10. We've cut together for
you all the points scored in
the match.'

*'Run
VT . . . 9-8-7-6-5-4-3-2-1-. Go
to it'*

The Paris tries and goals flash over the screen, eighty
minutes of rugby condensed in a twinkling by the skills of our
production assistants and videotape crew to less than a
minute. Still no JPR.

'10 seconds left'
'Stand by Cardiff. Cue Frank'

Still no JPR. I start talking to Gareth, who is as good as ever.
He's obviously added a few more of those good television
habits to his purse today. In London they start counting me
out of the programme. The titles are run off the clock, we're
never off early, never late.

A Grandstand Weekend

'3 minutes to cueing titles'

Halfway through Gareth, JPR is thrust into my eyeline, off camera. The team has cracked it again. On air, I call him in to join us, and we bid him farewell. Says he's going to concentrate on squash, at which he's already a formidable competitor. Somebody else's turn to feel the heat of a great sportsman.

'2 minutes to cueing titles'

He talks about his injury. A few more stitches, more or less, to hold his battered body together.

'1 minute to cueing titles'

I'm trying to leave nothing out, and lock my mind into getting out of the programme neatly and with dignity.

'Run titles'

I've ten seconds to fill. Ten seconds at the end of five hours of *Grandstand*. I have a handful of scores of my own in one hand: things I did right, plans that worked. In the other, the imperfections, the limitations, the inadequacies. Never mind, next time it'll be flawless.

Frank
'John Williams, thank you very much. Congratulations on today and on all the memories you've left us from a great career in rugby. That's it for today. From all of us on *Grandstand* – goodbye.'

*'Run end-titles . . .
9-8-7-6-5-4-3-2-1 . . .'*

When it's finished, it's marvellous. 'Thank you gentlemen' to the crew. 'Thank you London.' 'Thank you, Frank.' Unclip. I am free of the noise in my ear, ready to join the human race again, ready to face the Athletic Club.

The committee room is like some black hole of Calcutta; it is certainly the place to be. Old, braided, tasselled caps, belonging to past, revered heroes; sepia photographs of teams, sitting Edwardian style, serious, and some of their owners are actually still here. There are five members of a former Welsh scrum, still together, still comrades, packing down in the middle of the floor, showing how they did it twenty-five years ago. They rise and disentangle, displaying five sets of ears, still swollen, battered and misshapen, trophies in themselves. One leads the singing. The room heaves. This is a ritual they've enjoyed uninterrupted after the English matches for sixteen successive years. They're very generous in success. I'm spotted. Arm around my shoulder, vice-like. 'Never mind, boyo – come and have a drink.'

After a decent interval, I disentangle myself. Ally and I take our small *Grandstand* team to eat. The restaurant is Italian, but there's no way of avoiding celebrating Welshmen. With the menu, the waiter brings me a bottle of champagne. 'Compliments of Mr Max Boyce over there, sir.' Attached to the neck of the bottle is a note. 'Sorry you had to come second, Frank. I know, 'cos I was there.'

Postcript

A year later, another season, and in 1980 England are storming to their first Grand Slam for twenty-three years. They've beating the Irish and the French. Bill Beaumont's leadership and a splendid pack are exciting an enthusiasm for the English game that has been absent for years. This time the Welsh are at Twickenham, for the third match of England's series. I had a day off *Grandstand,* to enjoy the rare delight of experiencing the occasion without all the worry of the programme. Stephen came with me. We had lunch in the car park with friends. Again, there were great hopes that we could beat the Welsh, but this time the hopes were founded on real evidence that we had a fine team.

England did win that day, but I took no pleasure in it. Victory, instead of being sweet, was soured by a match that bristled with naked aggression and, almost, hate. We stood for the anthems, which were howled down with the most unhealthy venom by both sets of supporters. The first fifteen minutes were like a third world war, with early tackles, and boots and fists flying on both sides. This wasn't what we'd come for. Two fine teams were betraying the traditions, tampering with a great game and polluting it. Paul Ringer of Wales was sent off. England weren't playing at their best anyway, and Wales were down to fourteen men.

I sat next to a visiting Welshman; he was friendly but

critical. 'You've not got a very good side', he said. 'Yes, we have,' I replied, 'but they're not having a very good day'. As the game ebbed and flowed, violently, we were each in turn elated and cast down. Wales scored a try, very late on. My friend sat back happily, obviously convinced that all was as it should be – Wales were going to beat the English yet again. It did look that way. Then in the dying seconds, a penalty was given to England. It was wide-angled, out on the right. Dusty Hare, the England full-back, hit a beauty and Twickenham exploded.

I couldn't resist it. I turned to my neighbour, who was deflated and horror-stricken. 'What you have to remember at this precise moment', I said, 'is that sport is a shared experience, and that it's all for the good of the championships for the honours to pass around occasionally'. I don't think he saw my point.

So it was 9-8 to England – what merriment in the car park as the toasts were drunk. There was sadness, too, at the rough play, and resentment by the Welsh contingent, who deep down harboured the awful thought that if their team had kept its cool and played its normal skilful game, they'd have won in a canter. I agreed with that, but the victory was ours.

Passing the television vans on the way out an hour later, I spied a familiar figure with a few of his friends. It was Max Boyce, keeping a low profile. We embraced enthusiastically. It is always a delight to see him, and I tell you never more so than at that particular moment. He put a brave face on it.

'Frank', he said, 'it's the worst day of my life. We've lost here today. I discover that in the Football League, Wrexham have lost, so too have Swansea and Cardiff. I'm ringing Shropshire to ask if Shrewsbury is near enough to the Welsh border to count for us today!'

I introduced him to Stephen.

'Play rugby do you, boy?' he said. 'Now look here – you've got a Welsh mother, haven't you? Right, now you pick the right side d'you hear. You can't play for *them*!' – pointing at me.

'Never mind, Max', I replied. 'I've no champagne, but I'm sorry you had to come second. I know, Max, 'cos I was there!'

6

CAVALIER CRICKET

Of all the sports I've played, and/or enthusiastically followed, cricket has always been my first love. It is a game that embraces every mood, every emotion. It can be elegant – witness Garfield Sobers or Tom Graveney or Colin Cowdrey effortlessly stroking the ball to the boundary, the timing of bat against ball so exquisite that you hardly hear a sound as the two meet, yet the ball races away jet-propelled. It can also be violent! I once saw Colin Milburn looking like some village blacksmith clubbing – and clubbing is the word – the West Indian fast bowlers to the far corner of Lord's cricket ground and into the ducking crowd in the old grandstand. That was real violence.

Cricket can be unbearably exciting, too, like that 1971 Gillette Cup semi-final at Old Trafford with the gloom descending, nine o'clock approaching, and the lights on in Trafford Park railway station. The Lancashire batsmen were straining to reach the Gloucestershire total in the four remaining overs; David Hughes hit out ferociously to achieve a victory that will be remembered by all who saw it. A great many did, because although the earlier part of the game had been covered on BBC-TV, and later in the evening highlights were to be shown, normal scheduling was abandoned at 8.50pm, because unbelievably the match was still on. Paul Fox, then the Controller of BBC-1, postponed a Robert Robinson ten-minute letter programme, and over to the match we went. Exactly nine minutes thirty seconds later it ended, just enabling Jim Laker to round off a tremendous occasion and for the nine o'clock news to start dead on time! What a perfect day all round.

The first Gillette Cup competition started in 1963, at a time when cricket in England was at a pretty low ebb. The huge post-war crowds that had packed the Test match grounds, the Roses matches and Kent v Middlesex had drifted away. The pace of life had changed. No longer could people find the time to devote to a three-day championship match, and in any case the intellectuality of it, the tactics, the containment, seemed out of tune with a life that was accelerating and demanding new and more instant entertainment.

In 1965 Bryan Cowgill, BBC's Head of Sport, and Bagenal Harvey, a London agent who represented both broadcasters and many cricketers too, came up with the answer. Harvey had a strong tie with cricketers. In fact his business was born out of a friendship with Denis Compton. He had discovered that Denis, whose dashing improvisation on the cricket field, and an equally dashing 'Brylcreem-boy' image off it, was less than efficient in organising his professional life. 'His car', Bagenal once told me, 'was littered with unanswered correspondence going back months'. Their association grew into a mutually advantageous relationship, and as more cricketers, such as Ted Dexter and Jim Laker, realised the advantages of being able to concentrate on their cricket and leave the administration of their careers to Harvey, his business flourished. The International Cavaliers was formed, a cricket club with members from all over the world, top-class players who played largely for charity and other cricketers' benefits.

Sponsorship in sport was a growing influence too, and Bagenal sought to encourage it. Both he and Cowgill saw the possibilities. Cowgill was an immense competitor for the BBC. He was forging a dynamic, thoroughly professional, television sports empire, which at this time was growing rapidly with the arrival and development of the BBC's second channel. Cowgill wanted a regular cricket series. Some sort of match that he could televise from start to finish, a match that would attract a new cricketing public because they could see a beginning, a middle, and an end, without leaving the ground – unlike the ponderous, three-day championship games, where, if you were unlucky, you could invest a complete day and see only a contest that stultified into stalemate. What was needed was a format that would encourage the players to be aggressive in their approach, where the hitting of sixes would bring rewards, where the scoring of the series' fastest fifty and the taking of wickets by bowlers, rather than merely containing the run-rate, would put money into their pockets. Above all, it must be a series that would bring the crowds back to the game, but even more important, because Cowgill competed over every inch of life, it must get television viewers watching his programmes!

Cue Frank!

The ingredients were cleverly mixed. Cowgill had the television channel and the professionals to present the programme. Harvey had access to some of the world's finest players, many of whom were only seen in England every three of four years when they visited on an official Test match tour. He also had ideas about a sponsor. The trinity of BBC-2, the International Cavaliers, and Rothmans, the cigarette company, was born. The matches were to be played and transmitted live – on Sunday. How long were they to last? Gillette Cup cricket was sixty-five overs a side. That meant starting mid-morning, and, likely as not, continuing well into the evening: too long. Forty overs a side was decided upon, starting at 2pm. When estimates were made as to the finishing time, it became clear that some inroads would have to be made into the BBC's Sunday evening religious hour, or the God Spot, as it was called, which effectively started at 6pm. It had become tradition, and tradition had become law almost, that religious programmes should occupy the early part of Sunday evening. Cowgill needed to run his cricket into that hitherto sacrosanct area.

The BBC Governors had to be persuaded before such a dramatic, and to many, unthinkable, change could be made. They were reluctant, to say the least, but when it was pointed out that Garfield Sobers, or Tom Graveney, or Denis Compton, or the Nawab of Pataudi might well be at the wicket, opposition mellowed somewhat. Cricket, the game of manor house, village church, pub and village green, was clearly vital. The Governors persuaded themselves that the sight of a world-class batsman in full flow was as much an uplifting experience as *Songs of Praise,* and without doubt, to the greater glory of God!

A major obstacle had been overcome. There was another, in the form of cricket's establishment, who ran the game as of God-given right. In particular, they controlled the destinies of the seventeen English counties, the foundation of the game in this country, and the nursery from which the game's great players emerged to represent their country in Test matches – again controlled by Lord's. It was the counties who were needed to provide the opposition for the International Cavaliers.

At the time, cricket played on Sundays was strictly beer cricket. No county games were played, and charitable games were therefore arranged to help swell the pockets of those county professionals whose benefit year it was. It was strictly ya-hoo stuff. Batsmen bowled, bowlers batted, the game's extroverts fooled around, it was all very gentle, and not very well organised. The money they raised did not amount to very much, and one crucial element was lacking. Competition. If, the star attraction came to the wicket, he was allowed to display his talents without interruption – nobody bowled fast to him, catches were deliberately put down to keep him at the wicket and really it was a big yawn masquerading as entertainment. For Cowgill, the complete competitor, it was the last thing he wanted. His objective was a match, played for real, with rules that would encourage adventurous batting, aggressive bowling, mustard-hot fielding, and for money – the one thing that might persuade the players (who at that time were paid in washers and little else), to take it all seriously.

To start with, the counties took a lot of convincing that they should take part. It was a totally new concept, and also they were worried about being associated with a sponsor – that seems odd now, doesn't it, bearing in mind how cricket of all the sports has leapt into bed with Mammon? Most of all, they were extremely wary of a competition that was taking place completely outside the jurisdiction of the game's traditional rulers, the MCC at Lord's.

The idea was, and this was the clincher in the end, that the Cavaliers would play one game against each county in the season, plus one or two others, like Oxford and Cambridge Past and Present, to make up the required television series. Any profit should go to the relevant county's beneficiary that season, and the argument was that the Cavalier players would be such an attraction, and the game played so realistically, that the crowds would come and the money roll in. Some counties were persuaded; others said no, deciding to sit back and watch developments.

The first series began in 1965. It became a smash hit on the cricket grounds and on television, and there's no doubt in my mind it was the seed from which grew the highly popular and highly profitable limited-overs game we have today, in all its forms.

From a television point of view there were two particularly interesting innovations, as far as the cricket was concerned. The programmes were to have a presenter at the match. Someone who, in vision, would welcome viewers to the game, set up the characters, the personalities, and what is more talk to the players as they came off after an innings, or during the interval. This had never been done before. In Test matches, plus the Roses game between Yorkshire and Lancashire, which was about the only county three-day game televised, the commentator remained out of vision, purely as a commentator. An interview with a player, apart from possibly the England captain after the game, was unheard of. It was also decided that in the Sunday series we'd stay on the air during the tea interval, to talk to interesting people at the match – not necessarily the players – or to feature the ground, the county whose guests we were, the club's foundations and history. The presenter was also required to stage-manage the presentation of the winning cheque at the end, talk to the heroes of the day, and say goodbye.

Cowgill chose his producer well. Alan Mouncer, who'd come up through the BBC ranks, had been a BBC outside broadcasts cameraman. He was emerging as one of television's most imaginative producers of outside events, and he was given the job of launching the new series. The first presenter was Brian Moore, a newcomer to television, as he was working in BBC Radio sports department. Sadly for Brian, after his first programme, the very first match, his radio boss insisted he stayed with radio, so Frank Bough was wheeled in for the second Sunday game on BBC-2. That was the start of a close, seven-year association with cricket which gave me nothing but pleasure.

The Cavaliers really produced the goods when it came to the players. There were regular appearances from Garfield Sobers, surely the greatest all-round cricketer the game has ever seen. There were the Pollock brothers from South Africa, Graeme and Peter; little Hanif Mohammad, Lance Gibbs, the great West Indian off-spinner, and Rohan Kanhai of West Indies; the Nawab of Pataudi, captain of India; and Colin Bland of South Africa, a cover field of legendary speed and accuracy of throw. The Cavaliers brought new, untried talents to the series, too; for example a tall, gangling youth called Clive Lloyd from Guyana. And did the crowds come to see them play! In the early days of the series, the matches were played on lesser-known grounds, like Tichborne Park in Hampshire, the private ground at the home of Sir Anthony Doughty Doughty of Tichborne (yes, that really was his name!). The incumbent of the title agreed to an interview with me during the tea interval, recalling some of his early memories of country house cricket, of how his grandfather had been an immensely keen batsman, but was not so keen on hours spent fielding, so he used to send his valet out to field for him. As he sat there telling me the story, he was so huge he overflowed the deckchair on all sides, so I presumed he had continued the family tradition!

Another ground we were fond of visiting was Ascott, in Buckinghamshire (not the racecourse, Ascot), the home of the Rothschilds – a beautiful house, where the family hospitality to both cricket and television teams after the match was legendary. Ascott had a splendid private cricket ground where quite by accident I happened to come across one of the most elusive and unapproachable of the world's great oil men.

My in-vision position was usually just at the edge of the boundary line somewhere near the pavilion, where I could grab a quick word with the incoming batsmen – an innovation which could be either rewarding or disastrous, depending on how the batsman had performed. The first time Leicestershire had a fixture with the Cavaliers, Tony Lock, the great former Surrey and England spin bowler, was the Leicestershire captain. In Sunday matches of a charitable kind Tony had been accustomed to being treated equally charitably when he got to the wicket. At the least he would expect to receive a friendly ball to get him off the mark. He hadn't quite got the message about the new style, competitive, Sunday philosophy. He did that day though, because Sobers bowled him neck and crop first ball, and Tony was furious.

'How is it', I said, sticking a mike under his nose as he stormed past me, 'how is it?'

'How is it? What's going on out there? It's like a bloody Test match!'

We were making progress.

But at Ascott, I was sitting at my bench watching the match and keeping an eye out for a likely character to interview. We never used to miss a ball of the play, but talk through it and round it, and if the character was a knowledgeable cricketer the discussion generally produced a fascinating insight into the game. All of a sudden, a gentlemen casually walked up to the other end of the bench and sat down. He was a big, bearded man with an orchid in his button-hole: Nubar Gulbenkian, as large as life.

I decided to give it a go.

'Good afternoon', I said. 'Good afternoon', he replied. 'This is all exceedingly pleasant, what's it all about?'

'BBC-2 Sunday cricket match', I said. 'International Cavaliers against the Rest of the World.' (This was one of the extra fixtures on the list, because at this stage not all the counties had joined in.) I ploughed on. 'Mr Gulbenkian, isn't it?'

'Yes, that's right.' He seemed very pleasant, very amiable.

'Tell you what – while we're sitting here chatting, would you mind if we swung this camera on to us, so that the viewers can eavesdrop, as it were? No nasty questions, mind – all perfectly correct.'

'All right' he said, 'why not?'

I picked up what we called the 'lazy microphone' through which I spoke to Alan Mouncer, busily directing his cameras from the scanner van. 'Alan, end of this over – interview. Nubar Gulbenkian.'

He replied direct into my earpiece. 'Bloody hell – really? Right.'

The interview went something like this. 'With me here, watching the cricket, is Mr Nubar Gulbenkian. Good afternoon sir – are you fond of cricket?'

'Well, not particularly.'

'Just paying a visit then?'

'Well, as a matter of fact I came here to see Evelyn Rothschild for a meeting about the local Hunt in these parts, but there seems to have been some misunderstanding about the date, so seeing all this going on here, I was curious. What is going on here?'

'A cricket match', I said, feeling slightly foolish, 'between the International Cavaliers and the Rest of the World'.

'That sounds a very modest affair – who are they?'

'Well, that's Gary Sobers', I said, 'bowling now'.

'Who is he?' asked the great man.

I was in deep now. 'A very famous cricketer indeed – captain of the West Indies side.'

'And that one over there?', indicating.

'Graeme Pollock.'

'Who does he play for?'

'South Africa.'

'Really.'

I was sinking fast.

Suddenly he was pointing to the boundary line at our feet. 'What's that for?' he asked.

I got the feeling I was being taken for the most enormous

ride, but I wasn't exactly sure. 'Well', I found myself saying, 'if the ball rolls over that line four runs are scored, a boundary, and if the ball is struck clearly over the line then it's six.' By now I was in small pieces.

'Thank you', he said, 'that's most courteous of you'. He stood, and slowly walked away.

That feast of pavilion interviews enabled me to meet some great players. I remember that whenever I was in Taunton for a Somerset game, somebody would inevitably bring up the names of Arthur Wellard and Harold Gimblett. Now Harold I'd met and interviewed. He had been a tremendous hitter of a cricket ball, and had made more runs for Somerset at that time than anybody else, starting with a century in his first county game against Essex at Frome as a twenty-one-year-old. Amazingly, he didn't go in until number eight in the order, but then proceeded in a great hurry, presumably because he was worried about running out of partners, to hit 3 sixes and 17 fours in a total of 123. It was all over in 63 minutes and remained the fastest 100 of the year 1935. After the war he hit 310 against Sussex.

But the folks of Somerset spoke with even greater awe of Arthur Wellard, and him I'd never met. They spoke of his hitting – mighty pull drives, exactly timed, soaring into St James's Churchyard at one end of the Taunton Ground, and into the river at the other; of the summer in which he hit 72 sixes; of the two occasions on which he hit 5 sixes in one over. One of those occasions was in 1936, at Wells, against Derbyshire. Wellard took nine wickets with the ball, and then when the game looked lost he picked up the bat, and struck 7 sixes and 8 fours in an innings of 82 out of 102. His efforts produced a famous one-wicket victory. Wellard was clearly a legend, and after his playing days were over he disappeared to the south-east of England. His absence perpetuated and amplified the feats he had left behind.

One Sunday, in the third season of Cavalier competition, soon after I arrived at the Taunton ground several people spoke to me. 'He's here, you know.' 'Who?' I asked. 'Arthur', they said, 'Arthur Wellard. He's on a visit.'

I sought out the great man. It is always tricky meeting a legend. The legend is never the man so much as his feats, and since I'd never seen any of Arthur Wellard's great accomplishments I was able to talk easily to this exceedingly pleasant gentleman, who sat in front of a camera with me and no doubt stirred the blood of many who had actually seen his ferocious batting, as he recalled his career.

Armstrong of Derbyshire was the bowler who suffered to the tune of five sixes in one over from Arthur Wellard. The other was Frank Woolley of Kent. In fact, Wellard was missed off the sixth ball of the over and on the boundary at that! I interviewed Woolley at Maidstone. He was eighty years old and stood as straight as a ramrod. Here was one of cricket's great all-rounders, one of a very limited band of players gifted with both bat and ball. Nearly 59,000 runs and well over 2,000 wickets is a record that brooks no argument. He was a man clearly to be spoken of in the same breath as Sir Garfield Sobers. He sat so erect, was so slim and so fit for a man of his years that I felt really ashamed of my spreading waistline – and I was only half his age. I complimented him on how well he looked and in particular on the straightness of his bearing. 'Thank you, my boy', he said, smiling thinly. 'Fact of the matter is I've got a bit of trouble with my back – can't bend the thing at all'!

The commentary team varied. Sometimes it was Peter West or Trevor Bailey, sometimes Sir Learie Constantine – and what a gentleman he was. I sometimes picked him up and drove him to the matches. It was a real privilege to listen to him talking about the game, the players he'd played with, and his whole philosophy of cricket. I so wished I'd seen him play. Mostly though, the team was Jim Laker and John Arlott.

John gave me some of the most wonderful memories of Sunday cricket. A day with him was a real joy, and still is. I was first enchanted by him in Somerset, when on the Saturday evening before the game at Taunton, he invited Alan Mouncer and myself to dinner. He was staying at a delightful country inn, his regular watering-hole when he worked in Somerset. It was an old English pub, deep in the countryside, with rose garden, doves, the lot, just too good to be true. The landlord and his wife clearly adored him, and the three of us ate alone in the tiny, panelled dining-room. 'How many clarets shall I open, John?' asked the lady. 'Let's start with four', he said, 'and put 'em on the floor down here by my right hand'. His love of food and wine is boundless. Mostly he talked, while Alan and I listened. The soft Hampshire voice, known and loved all over the world where cricket is played, played with the words, assembling effortlessly the images he conjures so well, ranging over cricket and cricketers with deep affection. It was a most beautiful evening to be cherished.

But the real joy is to be invited to the Arlott household for the day. Assembly is 10.30am at The Old Sun at New Alresford, a former pub, and, at the time, John's home.'Well I've got to have somewhere to put the wine, haven't I? There's a very good cellar here.' The time is 10.30 because first on the programme is a round of golf, but not until after a glass of Berger and soda in the oak-floored, book-lined lounge. 'Gets where the brush cannot reach', says John, studying his glass. Then to the golf; not the eighteen-hole thrash of the true golf nut, but a neat nine holes, which takes us just nicely to the sherry (William and Humbert) before lunch. That *does* take longer than eighteen holes of golf! With lunch, a glass or two of white wine. 'Mere mouthwash' says the host. Then it is on to the claret. It is brought up from the cellar, several vintages, all beautiful examples of the French wine-grower's art. The wine is served in Victorian glasses, a fine accompaniment to the food, plain but delicious steak-and-kidney pie.

The afternoon grows richer. John is the perfect host, and if you enjoy his commentaries, imagine the lyricism of a private lunch party with him.

By now, astonishingly, it is 5pm. 'I'd like you all to see the cellar.' Down the hole we go, to one of the finest private collections of good wine in Britain. He's delighted, because the *Guardian* has just asked him to be its wine correspondent. 'I've finally outdone Neville Cardus', he exclaims gleefully. 'He wrote of the Halle Orchestra and of cricket at Old Trafford. Me, cricket and wine!' He points out the rack of half-bottles of champagne. 'Very nice occasionally with a kipper at breakfast.' By the time we emerge it is 6pm, and time for the William and Humbert again! The day has been so full of the quality of life.

Apart from his extraordinary way with the English language, John has a less widely-known talent: the ability to conjure food and drink out of the most barren of circumstances, and when I say British Rail on a Sunday evening, I really do mean barren. The Sunday game was at Cardiff. As was their habit, he and Jim Laker split the match between them, with John finishing his stint about an hour before the match ended at about 6.30pm. John didn't wait for it to finish, but simply said that he was going to the station to try and organise us some food on the evening train back to London.

The match and the programme ended, the small party of us

– producer, producer's assistant, Jim Laker and I, fled to Cardiff Station to catch the train. John was waiting for us inside the barrier as we went on to the platform. 'Right' he said. 'It's all fixed. We have to stand ready further along the platform', and he led us to a very precise spot. We all knew there was no restaurant on the train we were catching, but when the train came in and stopped, the restaurant car was right opposite us, otherwise deserted but for one table laid for dinner. We entered, sat down, and ham salad was served with half-bottles of wine to wash it down. Passengers moved past us, mystified at the strangely solitary dinner party. 'I rang back down the line to Swansea', John said. 'Here's to British Rail.' John retires this year, 1980, to the island of Alderney; a giant amongst broadcasters, to be heard no more.

All the time the Cavaliers were growing in popularity on BBC-2, and breaking down prejudices, largely because of the success of the series. At Huddersfield, where they'd given up playing championship cricket five years previously, the gates were closed on a huge crowd which had to be allowed to spill on to the outfield for safety's sake. At Edgbaston, which is a huge ground, Tom Cartwright's benefit day was a real landmark in that it attracted fifteen thousand people and Tom came out of the day with a huge contribution to his benefit fund. By this time the beneficiaries of those counties who had not joined in the Cavaliers' experiment were beginning to demand a Cavalier fixture. They were seeing what a tremendous boost it gave to the benefits elsewhere, and they wanted a slice of the action.

All this time I was being paid to spend my time watching a game I adore, a game that is usually played in very attractive surroundings, by a particularly pleasant and convivial gang of sportsmen. There was a lot of additional fun, beyond the cricket itself, as well. For example I had a memorable day in the apple orchards of Kent when Colin Cowdrey asked me down to the home of one of the county's friends and benefactors, where there was to be a fête to raise funds for and celebrate Kent's hundred years of playing county cricket. It was late May, and luckily a most beautiful day. I parked my car under the apple blossom, and made my way to the house. There was plenty of food and drink, and very good company. The county tennis team were there as well as the county cricketers. It was all wonderfully English.

During the afternoon, Colin said 'Look, the Kent players

Above: On a Thames river boat in 1977, at the Maidenhead Jubilee Regatta. (Maidenhead Advertiser)

Below: Grandstand preparation – (left) a quick flick with the powder puff, and (right) synchronise watches . . . worry, worry, worry. Bearded graphics man John Tidy is in the background.

Above: With Bing Crosby on *Grandstand:* he put money on Uncle Bing, the horse, and it won.

Below: With HRH Prince Charles, immaculately dressed for his Jubilee appearance on *Nationwide*.

Above: The other side of the *Grandstand* studio cameras – what the viewer doesn't see. Note the two monitors for me to watch in front, as well as the one beside me.

Below: The BBC's 1979 General Election team. From my left, Donald McCormick, John Timpson, David Dimbleby, Bob Mackenzie, Brian Redhead, Libby Purves, Robin Day, and Jimmy Young, on the steps of All Souls, Portland Place, London.

Above: A proud moment – HRH Princess Anne presents me with BAFTA's Richard Dimbleby Award for 'the year's outstanding contribution to factual television', in March 1977. (Michael Barrett)

Below: A family gathering in our present house in Maidenhead. From left to right, Andrew, Nest, Stephen and David. (B. Norman)

are going to do a little turn, and give an exhibition down there on the tennis court. Would you mind taking the public address microphone, making the introductions and giving a little commentary? It'll help make the thing go with a swing.'

The hard tennis court was in a hollow, so the crowds gathered all round as Cowdrey and his team went through their paces, batting and fielding and pulling out all the professional party tricks that people enjoy so much. Great applause. Then Colin rejoined me, took the microphone, and issued an invitation to anyone who would like to bowl at him. 'And I think Frank Bough here should start us off', he said.

There were hundreds of people watching, packing the banks all round as I went down on to the court and took the ball. England's cricket captain took guard at the other end, with that easy, relaxed stance, right out of the coaching manual. The stumps, by the way, were the kind that are always used on a hard surface, spring fitted to a firm base, so that they rock to and fro. I'd played a lot of cricket, nothing very grand mind, for my school, for my college at Oxford, and for local clubs. I was an all-rounder, so I thought I knew what a good length was, and usually bowled straight. The next few seconds were sheer magic, and I'll be boring my grandchildren with the story. Up to the wicket I went, with ten swift strides, and over went the arm.

Now, although I say it myself, it was a very good ball! It didn't do a lot in the air, and the tarmac meant there was little help from the wicket, as it were. But it was straight on a length, just about middle and off, and the England captain missed it! Whack! The stumps rocked, the crowd roared and I felt ten feet tall. Afterwards he said 'Very well bowled', looking me straight in the eye, and the truth dawned. 'Now look', I said. 'Don't say another word. Don't you dare tell me you let that go through on purpose – I'll never speak to you again. I've just bowled one of the world's great batsmen and that's all I want to remember!' Cowdrey smiled.

The man can be so thoughtful, too. There was that day, as part of the fund-raising, the auction of an iced cake. It was a very special iced cake, a big one, flat, and with a miniature cricket match being played on it. It had tiny figures, wickets, a scoreboard, and a little frame all the way round as a boundary rail. All was set in green icing, a testimony to some fond lady supporter's culinary skills. The following week our second son, Stephen, had a birthday, and I set my heart on winning the cake to give him a special present. I also wanted to make my contribution to the day. So I bid well, and the cake was mine.

When it was time to leave, Colin came over to me. 'Thanks for lending your presence', he said. 'We very much appreciated it and we'd like you to have this', and he handed me a small cricket bat, autographed by all the county players. I was having quite a day! As I loaded the cake carefully into the boot, he remarked, 'You were very determined on the cake', and I explained to him that Friday of the next week was Stephen's birthday, and that's why I had wanted it.

I drove home full of the joys of life. I'd got my bat, my cake, and what is more the memory of that moment when the stumps rocked and Cowdrey walked. Ten days later, on the morning of Stephen's birthday, a telegram arrived: 'Dear Stephen, many happy returns of the day. Hope you enjoy the cake. Colin Cowdrey.'

Friendships were made all round in cricket. At Leicestershire, for example, where the county club was in the process of being dramatically face-lifted by a young man called Mike Turner, the secretary/manager. He had a vision of turning a workaday Midlands ground at Grace Road, Leicester, into an international cricket arena. As I write, twelve years or so later, he is about to succeed. The new pavilion, the accommodation, the facilities for members and public are so vastly improved there that the place is unrecognisable from the dreary ground it was in the mid-sixties. Mike, and Charles Palmer, the chairman, have done for Leicester what Clough and Taylor have done for Derby County and Nottingham Forest. Under their guidance, the Leicester County Club has enjoyed its most successful year since its foundation, both on and off the field. Mike cornered me (in the nicest possible way) into becoming a member, and also into making a speech or two at their fund-raising dinners. It is always a pleasure to visit Grace Road.

Many happy days were spent, too, in the company of the Glamorgan players. Living so close to Wales as a boy, and having a Welsh wife, has meant that I've always enjoyed visits to the Principality. When Tony Lewis, their captain, after a Sunday game at Swansea asked me if I'd like a memorable evening, that was one invitation I couldn't resist. The tradition was apparently to go up to Pontardulais where the local rugby club's watering-hole was a small pub called

Cavalier Cricket

The Fountain. What a night of generous hospitality and music-making we had, with the Welsh leading the chorale, as only they can.

A year later, Kent were the visitors oddly enough, and both teams set off up the valley in the evening. Since my last visit, the rugby club had moved into spanking new headquarters, and the place was heaving with people. As we went in, we all bought raffle tickets for the big monthly draw. First prize was a handsome Wedgwood table lighter. Halfway through the evening, the secretary asked me if I'd mind going on stage and introducing the visitors from Kent. It is always happening this, part of the penalty of my profession I suppose!

So up I went, and called out the Kent players: Colin Cowdrey, Alan Knott, Derek Underwood. There was great applause and a real Welsh welcome. 'While we have Mr Bough up here', says the secretary, 'I wonder if he'd be so good, since he's clearly an impartial observer, to make the draw for our big monthly raffle.' A huge Kelloggs cornflakes container was produced, brimful with tickets. They'd been selling them for weeks. I thrust my hand deep inside. 'Blue ticket 426', I bellowed above the din, and waited for the inevitable shouts of success from some lucky winner. Nothing. Again: 'Blue ticket 426.' Nothing. 'Come on, fellas, we haven't got all night. Can't hold up the proceedings any longer.' Nothing.

A thought occurred to me. I dived into my pocket for the tickets I'd bought on the way in. Hell! There it was – blue 426. 'You're not going to believe this', I said. They stamped and howled and gave me the full treatment: 'Fix, fix.' 'Why was he born so beautiful, why was he born at all. He's no bloody use to anyone . . .' etc, etc. 'I'll re-draw.' They wouldn't have that at all, and to howls of good-natured derision, I was presented with that beautiful blue Wedgwood table lighter. A week later, the top fell off. It was an imitation. They'd won in the end!

There was no doubt that in a very convivial cricketing community, Glamorgan seemed to have more parties than most. At the end of one season, on the last day of the Sunday series, I was invited to a celebration they were having to mark the end of cricketing hostilities. Glamorgan were playing Sussex at Hove on that last day, and there was to be a joint party in Brighton after the match. The televised game that day was at The Oval, which I was linking, so I planned to drive down to the south coast after I'd finished. Now when it comes to women, cricketers are as sharp as anybody in spotting a good one, and I discovered that Fanny Cassidy, the producer's assistant who worked with us on the Cavaliers' series, had been invited as well. No surprise, as Fanny is a very dishy lady indeed. I offered to drive her down from The Oval to the party, but said that I couldn't bring her back, because I'd booked a hotel room in Brighton for the night. Quite clearly the drink was going to flow freely, and there was no way I was going to climb into my car and drive back after a thrash like that. She agreed, and said that she too would stay in Brighton overnight. We drove down to the party. Whether it was because it was at the end of a long, sociable season or not I don't know, but for some reason the party didn't take off. It was pleasant enough, very convivial, but when midnight came I'd had very little to drink and decided that I'd abandon my plan to stay overnight and drive home after all. I found Fanny, said I had decided now to go back, and would drop her off in London if she liked. Her party hadn't gone too well either, so we left together.

At one in the morning, driving north up the A23 with this delicious lady alongside me, I suddenly started laughing. 'Do you know what, Fanny? They'll never believe me! Here am I, driving you *out* of Brighton of all places, in the small hours, with rooms booked at the Royal Albion. They'll never believe me.' They never have, either!

Actually I like to think that Fanny Cassidy and the other girls who worked in the scanner with the producer helped to break down some of the traditional prejudices that existed towards women in cricket. Historically, it is, or was, a game in which women had to know their place, and stay in it. At that time in the 1960s, whole pavilions, on the big grounds particularly, were banned to women, and for a woman to be seen in a long room or a members' bar or a committee room was unknown. In the Sunday version of the game, I was very keen indeed, as we all were, to encourage families to watch cricket together. It seemed to me that a cricket ground was such a pleasant place to be that the whole family – Mum, Dad and the children – could all enjoy being there together. Even if Mum wasn't particularly keen on the game, she could sit comfortably and relax, enjoy the sunshine, have tea, and be part of the family day out. Mind you, a great many women did learn to enjoy the game on Sundays. The format was simple, forty overs a side, and avoided many of the complications that are an essential part of the three-day game.

As for the youngsters, the more of them we could encourage to attend the matches at the grounds, the better for the future health of the whole game. I, for one, happily broke one of the cardinal rules of competitive television in this respect. Competitively, my job is to encourage people to stay glued to their sets, to watch my programme and nobody else. But on Sundays, if the weather was in doubt, I'd come up at 1.50pm when the programme started, tell the viewers that the game was on and actively encourage those who were anywhere near the ground to switch off, get off their backsides, and come to watch the cricket at the ground. It was to the benefit of both cricket and television, after all. We certainly didn't want to televise sport taking place in front of half-empty stands and terraces.

But what is the good of the whole family coming to a match, only for Mum and daughter to discover that they're not allowed into large areas of the ground, the best parts too, because they're only open to men? This caused a lot of anger early on in the series, with so many people coming to cricket for the first time, but happily nearly all the counties realised they had to move with the times. Although today there's still the odd corner where the male chauvinist pigs can gather away from the women, most grounds are open to both sexes.

I always took the line that if there were girls working on the television team with me, then where I went, they went. There was the odd kerfuffle when I'd simply say to the guardian of the hallowed ground, 'If she can't come in here, then neither shall I', and we'd have lunch out together somewhere else. There were some memorable breakthroughs though, notably at Southampton, where tradition was strong and where unfortunately lunch had been laid on for the television team in the committee room, the holy of holies, where no woman had ever trod. Not only did we bludgeon our way through with Fanny Cassidy, when we got to the hallowed committee table where lunch was, we insisted she sat in the chairman of Hampshire Cricket Club's great oak seat. When John Arlott, a Hampshire man to the bottom of his claret glass, walked in, he stood speechless, for the only time I ever remember. Eventually he spluttered: 'Fanny, Fanny – you're historic!' And sat down beside her.

One of the great joys of the series was to meet nearly all of the game's great players. Some were currently playing, of course, but I'm thinking mainly of those who have long since given up the game, but are still living legends: players like Sir Len Hutton, Godfrey Evans and Denis Compton.

We had decided early on in the Cavaliers' series that we would not go off the air and play gentle music during the tea interval. Instead, we'd explore the great well of cricket nostalgia in people, places and events. One summer, for example, we did a whole series about the famous grounds and pavilions, the long rooms, with their old bats and prints and old cricket balls with which great feats of bowling had been done, mounted and plated. This was when John Arlott came into his own. At tea, we'd wheel one of the cameras into the pavilion, and John would lead us round the walls and the showcases, never lost for a tale, a piece of history, a record. He was extraordinary, the amount he knew, and the stories were completely spontaneous. I remember once, when it rained at Trent Bridge, rather than put up the 'play delayed' caption to a musical accompaniment, John gave us a complete conducted tour of the past greats of Nottinghamshire cricket.

I think the end of the Cavaliers' series finally came one Sunday at Lord's. As the series exploded in popularity, the small village and country house grounds, and even the smaller county grounds like Taunton and Southampton, became increasingly inadequate; the greater capacity of Test match venues, like Edgbaston and Old Trafford, became essential. Finally it was decided to ask if we could play a game at that loveliest of arenas, Lord's cricket ground itself.

The authorities there finally consented. Our planning and organisation team, from Cavaliers, Rothmans and the BBC, now with a well-honed procedure for laying on the matches, leapt into action. Lord's was unimpressed. 'We'll have just three gates open', they said. 'But that's not enough. Thousands will turn up', we replied. 'Look, we know how many people watch cricket at Lord's on Sunday', they said. 'If you get five thousand, you'll be lucky.'

They remained unconvinced, until on the day fifteen thousand fans started laying siege to the place; extra gates had to be opened, and gatemen rushed in to man them. Lord's watched with amazement. All this had been going on outside their jurisdiction. They woke up at last. A new Sunday League competition was formed, the Cavaliers being excluded, and a new sponsor was found.

Cavalier Cricket

The Cavaliers are now remembered with affection only by those who were charmed by their cricket over those three years. Yet to them cricket owes the one-day game as we know it today – the John Player League, the Benson and Hedges Cup, the Prudential World Cup international games – all of which are such an essential economic prop to the modern game of cricket. The BBC, the Cavaliers, and Rothmans had the idea. They made it work, they were the pioneers, and they've been given precious little credit. I am delighted to have played a small part in what I believe to have been a major turning point in the history of the game.

7

POT-POURRI

Most of the disadvantages of being a telly face – and believe me, there are many – affect the family, the ones you love, and there are times when for their sake I fervently wish that I could just fade into total obscurity. For eleven months of the year I am prepared to be pinched and prodded as though I am a piece of topside, and talked about as though I wasn't there. 'Oh, he's quite ordinary, isn't he', said one dear old lady to another. (Standing right beside me, she was, too.) Well, I am. I've got two legs, two arms, a mortgage, a wife, and three sons. I've also developed a very chatty way of disentangling myself from an unsought conversation in one minute flat, without being rude to the person involved, so that they don't tell their friends that Frank Bough's a rude old bugger – couldn't even be bothered to pass the time of day. Nest says she can almost hear the click as I 'switch on' and gabble away, becoming the sort of person people seem to expect. It amounts to changing up a gear, I suppose: I must stop picking my nose and smile sweetly.

The most difficult part of the year is the other month – the one which you resolve to give entirely to the family – The Holiday. Even so, when you've disappeared to what you fondly believe is a remote corner of Europe, and the beach is empty, as sure as eggs is eggs, someone will appear from behind the nearest rock and enthusiastically canvas your views on Leeds United's chances of winning the championship. 'I feel if only they can stiffen up the defence a bit, and get a bit more punch into attack, they'd be world beaters, Frank.'

Of course, sport and television generally are everybody else's pleasure, their relaxation. They are mine, too, but they are also my business – and I do like to get away from them from time to time. But I'm being churlish. There are so many good things about my job as well. Walk into a room, and I am everybody's friend – at least, people will *talk* to me, even if it is only to complain that their sport isn't getting enough air time, or to ask why *Nationwide* is so left wing or right wing, or biased against or for abortion, or the unions or big business. I have long since discovered that impartiality is a total myth. It depends entirely on where you're standing. If anything, impartiality means that you agree with the other fellow's point of view.

Many deliciously unexpected things have happened to me in my job, too, and I've been places that I'd never have seen in any other profession. I had, for example, a truly profound experience in Wakefield, on a summer evening visit to the jail there.

One of the prison staff, who was trying to lighten the lives of the men who spend a large part of their lives there, had written to ask if I would go up one evening and talk to a group of the prisoners who were interested in sport. Every so often he would invite somebody up to do this, or show a few films. That kind of invitation I can never refuse. In the late afternoon I drove up from the south. Wakefield is not a pretty town, and the prison certainly doesn't do much for it; it is a bleak, awful pile, old and outdated. When they lock you up in Wakefield, it tends to be for a long stay. Most inmates have murdered somebody, yet, as the governor told me, 'I could let eighty per cent of these lads out tomorrow, absolutely certain in the knowledge that they'd never do it again. Usually they're here because they found the wife in bed with some-body else.' Ironically, the prison is situated in Love Lane.

I parked my car in the prison officers' car park, on rising ground on the other side of the lane opposite the grim prison gates. I rang the bell. Credentials were produced. Admitted. The staff I met were delighted to see me. Fifty or so men were gathered in a hut; most of them murderers. I launched out into my patter – stories of this and that – and then showed them some film, an edit of my favourite Cup Final which is Sunderland beating Leeds in 1973, against all the odds, when Sunderland were in the second division.

Within minutes, the prisoners were just another audience. The questions could have come from a Round Table dinner or the Institute of Engineers. 'How did you get into television? What is David Coleman – Eddie Waring – Harry Carpenter – like? (Always refuse to discuss colleagues.) Why do we have to have so much horse racing on the box? What else do you do the rest of the week? Why do you crucify referees with slow motion replays? Why does *Match of the Day* always show London clubs?' (If I'm in the south, this question is always the other way round – surely a good sign that Alec Weeks, our football boss, is on the right lines!) 'Why can't you give us more speedway?' Then, 'What is it like for you, Frank Bough, standing up there in this place, talking to us?'. That one almost floored me: below the belt.

By 7.30pm I'd finished. The evenings are short in Wakefield Prison. After recreation, they were all locked in their cells again by 8pm – and 8pm precisely. But there is time, said my host, to go and see the tropical fish man of Wakefield Prison.

The constant aim, you see, is to reduce the tension. The place is crowded, tempers fray, life, such as it is, sits heavily on every shoulder. There are two television sets, one switched permanently to BBC, the other switched permanently to ITV. There can be no argument, therefore, about what to watch: and therefore no tension. Something to do might be table tennis, which is vigorous and energetic, and works a bit of frustration out of the system; or it might be something soothing, gentle, calming, and beautiful, such as fish, glimmering, colourful, tropical fish. They breed more tropical fish in Wakefield Prison than anywhere else in Britain: tank upon tank of them, from eggs to thousands of tiny young fish, to beautifully constructed show-cases containing fully-grown fish of every conceivable shape, pattern and colour. All move soothingly through a tropical coral paradise – lovingly constructed from polystyrene. The Fish Man of Wakefield is proud of his kingdom. It's his life.

'That one there', he said, pointing proudly to a magnificent tank which was clearly the show-piece, 'holds pride of place in the Royal Yorkshire Show at Doncaster'.

'Great shame you never saw it there', I said. I bit my tongue.

'Oh, but I did', he said. 'Governor said – you've put it all together – only you can set it out to its best advantage. Go and see it properly displayed.'

He'd gone to Doncaster. 'It looked very good', he said, immensely pleased. You knew he could still see it there, in his mind's eye.

At eight o'clock it was time to go: lock-up time at Wakefield Prison. I'll never forget it. I walked down the centre of one of the cell-blocks, which splay out from a central hub like the legs of a cartwheel. It is several storeys high, with wire mesh above, and rows of doors just a few feet apart on either side. As I started the walk, there were men's voices everywhere, as if I was running a sort of verbal gauntlet – but a most friendly one. 'Hello, Frankie boy – what you doin' here then?' Clang, door closed. 'Hello Frank – enjoyed that Finnegan fight – used to do a bit meself, you know.' Fists up, sparring. Bang, door closed. 'Look, Boughy boy, tell that Jimmy Hill to show us some football when we can watch it.' 'Sure, I'll do that.' Clang, door closed. And so on and so on went the chorus, right down the block, just like any high street: quips, jibes, good humour. God know how, or why. At the end of the row I turned round and looked back. The place was deserted. Lock-up time at Wakefield Prison was complete.

As I left the prison, and those big gates closed behind me, it was still light, a warm summer evening. I took a deep refreshing breath, the air clear of the carbolic, body-sweat atmosphere inside. I suddenly appreciated what freedom was; and don't we take it for granted. Love Lane was quiet. I crossed the road and began to walk up the rise to where I'd left my car. 'Goodbye, Frank' rang out from somewhere behind me. I turned and looked back at the prison, at the rows and rows of cell windows visible over the high wall. Which one, I wondered? There was no way of telling. I waved generally and exaggeratedly. Through the still evening air came the call, as clear as a bell. 'See you Saturday, Frank.' I'll never forget that.

* * * * *

Nationwide once asked me to go to the Palladium to interview Bing Crosby. He was making one of his infrequent visits to London, where, as an old man now, he packed that huge theatre every night for a week.

I had met the maestro before. He'd been delightfully accommodating, talking to me and the viewers on *Grandstand* in the intervals between our various events. On and off for a couple of hours he had talked about anything and everything: Grace Kelly, Sinatra, Hope, and his love of sport, particularly golf. An extraordinary thing happened, too. He loved horse racing and took particular interest in the meeting we were covering that day. As we came to our second race, there in the list of runners was a horse called Uncle Bing. It was pure coincidence, but if there was ever a good reason for a bet that was it. 'Is there someone here who can put me a few pound notes on that one?' he asked. Amongst the studio team on *Grandstand* there is no shortage of people who like a flutter. In fact every Saturday afternoon a little sweepstake is orga- nised, known as The Swindle. Our out-of-vision readers, Len Martin and Tim Gudgin, are very much in charge, with the help, of course, of our racing sub-editors. Len Martin came over to the desk, and Bing gave him a five pound note. 'On the nose, please. That's most kind of you.' Uncle Bing romped home. The Old Groaner was delighted. Len Martin came over with his winnings and asked Bing if he'd sign the five pound note. Len had stood the bet out of his own pocket, and I know that Bing Crosby's own note, signed by the maestro himself, is one of Len's prized possessions. He'll need to be on very hard times indeed before that one will be used to pay the rent!

In preparation for my Palladium interview with Bing, due on the Wednesday, I decided I'd go and see the show earlier in the week to get something of the atmosphere of his perform- ance. So on the Monday I went along after my *Nationwide* programme and joined a full house, buzzing with anticipation. All of them were Crosby fans, on his side before he even appeared. When he did it was totally without fuss – there was no fanfare or big build-up. He just stepped neatly from the wings, a dapper, slim figure; only his face gave away his age, the skin like stretched parchment. 'Good evening', he said. The Palladium roof lifted several inches. I grew up with Sinatra, Nat King Cole and Crosby, and that soft, gentle voice, filled the big theatre, as familiar as an old friend. He had obviously tailored his vocal ambitions to suit his ageing vocal chords, so nothing he attempted was beyond his range. He was good, very good. *High Society, Blue of the Night*, even *White Christmas*, the old favourites washed over the audience and they adored it. As a finale, he performed a selection of phrases and choruses from fifty-eight songs – a feat of memory and professional stagecraft that couldn't be faulted. Encores and fervent applause marked the end of a remarkable event.

On Wednesday, interview night, I took Nest along with me. I had such a tremendous feeling of occasion that I wanted her to share it too. This time, of course, I went backstage, where I reintroduced myself to him in his dressing-room. 'Hey' he said, his memory working well. 'How's that Uncle Bing? What a horse that was!'

He agreed to do the interview in his dressing-room during a

fifteen-minute slot occupied by Ted Rogers, the comedian with him on the show. That in itself was a compliment. I know that if I am involved in a programme, such is the concentration needed that I would find it impossible to break off halfway through and accommodate somebody else as he was doing. I asked if we could stand in the wings to see his entrance. 'Sure, sure' he said. Nest and I went down to the stage level, and stood in the wings, glueing ourselves to the wall to keep out of the way and avoid distracting him.

It is fascinating to see how people gear themselves up to a public performance. Before a programme I have an irritating habit, irritating to others that is, of pacing around, being unbearably jovial and rather noisy. That is how I get myself warmed up, how I work myself up to the pitch where I know all my faculties are working properly. It drives Bob Wellings mad. His method is quite the opposite; he gets quieter and quieter. 'Noisy bugger' he'll mutter from across the studio, as I'm going through my routine. I have got into the habit of warning him now: 'Time to be noisy, Bob – sorry.' (Grunts from Mr W.)

Well, it was immensely reassuring to discover that even a distinguished international star like Crosby, legend that he was, still had to work himself up to a performance, yet he appeared, as he always did, totally relaxed on stage. As Nest and I watched, he paced around nervously, never still, going through his scales. 'Ba ba ba-ba ba-ba – ba-ba baa.' The old vocal chords were protesting somewhat, but Bing reminded them that once more it was time for a Crosby performance. It was a beautiful few moments, just him, Nest, and me. The stage manager appeared – 'Stand by, Bing' – the tabs opened, a quick shrug of the shoulders, and from the wings I then witnessed the same blindingly effective appearance on stage that only the much-loved greats of show business can achieve, exactly the same performance that I'd seen from the stalls three days earlier. The Palladium roof lifted once again.

At the interval, we were waiting for him in his dressing-room. He gave me a crisp, considerate, and charming fifteen-minute interview, and then slipped out again for his next spot. What a performer.

Four days later on a golf course he collapsed and died of a heart attack. Mine was the last television interview he ever gave.

* * * * *

Cue Frank!

My first visit to the Bristol Studios of the BBC shouldn't have been a particularly memorable one, but it turned out to be so. When the day began I wasn't going there at all, but to a very swish country club several miles outside the city of Bristol, to make a speech and present some trophies to a sportsman's lunch there. I really do enjoy that kind of occasion. I suppose the ham in me wants to see the whites of their eyes and to hear a laugh or two occasionally, after all the hours I spend gazing into a round, impersonal, television camera lens, which produces no human reaction at all. The way my professional life has developed, I spend a great deal of time in a television studio, presenting programmes, and that prevents me from actually attending events and meeting personally the people we feature in action. So I take every opportunity I can to get out and meet people.

At this particular lunch there was an excellent attendance of West Country sporting personalities, and I enjoyed it immensely. By about half past two, when I'd done my turn and handed over the pots, I began to say my farewells prior to driving back home down the M4. Suddenly I was called to the telephone in the club reception area. On the other end was a fairly agitated gentleman who introduced himself as a BBC producer in Bristol. 'We've never met', he said, 'and I'm sorry to bother you, but I'm in a bit of a hole and I wonder if you'd be able to help?'.

Well – a professional *cri de coeur* from a colleague, even though he's a stranger, is something to be taken seriously. 'Fire away – what can I do?' I replied.

'It's like this', he said. 'I'm due to record two programmes this afternoon in Bristol and one of the guests has failed to turn up. I can't possibly go ahead without somebody who is a telly face, and I was hoping that since you were in the area, you might have an hour or two free to take his place and get me off the hook.'

He really had problems. Very often when a series of programmes is being recorded, it makes good sense to do two of them on the same day. It is very much more economical, the studio and the camera crew and production team are all there, and a studio is tied up for only half the time. Here he was with all his finely-balanced plans in grave danger of collapse because his studio guest, one man, had failed to turn up. I was free, so of course I told him I would come. 'I've never been to the BBC Studios in Bristol', I told him, 'so a few directions could help speed me to you more quickly'.

He began to describe what seemed to be a pretty complicated journey into Bristol and across the city.

'Hang on', I said. 'I'm sure there must be someone leaving this lunch who's going that way, and can lead me to you.' I was about to put the phone down and find a guide, when I suddenly realised that in the panic I hadn't asked the most important question of all. 'What do you do by the way? What's the programme we're talking about?'

'Oh, sorry', he said. 'I'm the producer of *Going for a Song.*'

Well, in the Bough household we do collect the odd knick-knack, but as for really knowing anything about antiques, forget it. By now, though, I was in up to my neck. 'OK' I said. 'But on your own head be it. I'll be with you as soon as I can', and rushed off to find somebody to lead me to BBC Bristol.

Talk about neck. Roughly an hour later, with the videotape machine recording, I was sitting next to Arthur Negus, holding up a piece of glassware, pursing my lips as authoritatively as I could, saying 'Well Arthur, I'd put that at about 1860 or so, worth today, say – well – about £900?'! However, I did have a delightfully unexpected opportunity to meet Mr Antiques himself, Arthur Negus, and discovered with great pleasure that the man off camera is exactly the same as the man we see on our television screens – gentle, amusing, and fascinating to listen to. The problem was, I wanted to talk to him about antiques, while he wanted to talk to me about sport, in particular Aston Villa football club. He is a real fan of theirs, a very enthusiastic one. It never ceases to surprise me how a love of sport crosses all other boundaries.

The other joy that day was to meet another guest on the programme, the delicious Felicity Kendal of *The Good Life.* We competed against each other for the pleasure of taking home a little silver-plated cruet set. Sadly she got three answers right to my two, so she walked off with the prize!

* * * * *

Actually, being invited to appear on somebody else's show is always very flattering, but if you're a straight man like me in sport and in news and current affairs, you have to be very careful you are not made to look too much of a fool. Oddly enough, two of the funniest men in television never let you down in this respect, indeed an invitation to appear on a Morecambe and Wise Christmas show is something like a royal command performance. I have been lucky enough to receive the summons on two occasions, an honour indeed. Eric and Ernie have a quite uncanny knack of taking the mickey out of you, without denting your straight image in any way whatsoever. I know of nobody else who could possibly have persuaded that sexy, sexy superstar, Shirley Bassey, to wear army boots – but they did, and Miss Bassey lost none of her dignity or status. André Previn, Glenda Jackson, Elton John, have all been teased unmercifully by the pair of them and yet survived intact.

To work with Morecambe and Wise is to understand a little the enormous challenge it is to create something that makes people laugh. You begin to understand why comedians such as Tony Hancock, Max Wall and Mike Yarwood have all had to suffer dreadful depression and feelings of inadequacy in pursuit of what they believe to be ultimately the most rewarding aim of show business. There are a lot of people who can raise a guffaw with an elbow on the bar and a couple of pints of warming ale inside them. Try doing that at 10am, stone-cold sober on a Monday morning, in a dreary rehearsal room in Acton; it's another world. The comedian's life is hours of grinding professional repetition, honing and polishing, putting a line in here, an extra bit of business there, ruthlessly cutting out something that seemed a splendid gag at the time of creation but just doesn't work in practice. It is an enervating, draining process, when hours of rehearsal and preparation are needed for something that on the screen might last for no longer than a minute or two.

Such was the preparation for a dance routine that was to be part of this Morecambe and Wise Christmas show. The star guest was Glenda Jackson, a monumental actress and a much more than passable stand-in for Ginger Rogers in the proposed take-off of a Hollywood musical in the grand style. The sweeping staircase, the balustrades, the chandeliers, were all there, with Eric and Ernie top-hatted and tail-coated doing the Fred Astaire bit. Ernie had a walking cane that got longer as the routine developed, and which threatened to propel Miss Jackson to the far boundary of Shepherd's Bush. There was also a male chorus line. And what a chorus line: never before had so many uncoordinated incompetents been assembled on one dance floor at the same time. Combatants included Patrick Moore, Mr Universe, shaped somewhat like Jupiter anyway, his top hat and tails fitting where they touched, which wasn't very often; Eddie Waring, who knows a good Rugby League side-step when he sees it, but is to ballroom dancing what Arthur Scargill is to the aristocracy; Michael Parkinson – at least he had the figure for it, but he had an unfortunate habit of waving his cane around like a cricket bat; and then there was me.

'You were never lovelier' the music went. We moved as best we could, our backs to camera. 'Lovelier, lovelier, lovelier, lovelier . . . ' One by one we did the big turn to camera, with the tooth-parted smile – hams, all of us.

The great touch that Eric and Ernie have is that they never overplay. I think we were each recognisable in-vision for no more than three seconds. It was enough – quite enough! Seriously, though, the point had been made, and didn't need flogging to death. The whole routine lasted no more than five minutes, yet we were there from dawn until dusk before Eric and Ernie and John Ammonds, the producer, were satisfied: perfectionists all.

A year or two later the summons came again. A slightly different cast of characters was to appear this time. I was still there, and so too was Eddie, plus Michael Aspel, film buff Barry Norman, and news readers Peter Woods and Richard Baker. This time the producer was Ernest Maxim, famous for his choreography skills; he was going to have to call on every bit of his skill to coax that lot into action. 'Right gentlemen – the challenge is *There Is Nothing Like a Dame.'*

We all went pale, which is about the only thing we were ever to do in unison. Anybody who has seen *South Pacific* and that incredibly athletic dance sequence, with American sailors leaping and cavorting in every possible direction on a Pacific beach, will understand how we found the prospect. For days we assembled at Acton, where the rehearsal room rocked to the thunder of overweight middle-aged bodies, swearing and groaning as long neglected muscles were coaxed for 'one more time'.

We learnt a sequence of basic soft-shoe shuffle steps, all the while wondering when the real gymnastics were to start. One day four extremely young, slim, energetic professional dancers joined in, and the recording that millions of viewers watched that Christmas is a real tribute to the imagination of Ernest Maxim and the technical wizardry of the BBC's videotape editors. The sequence was so beautifully cut together that even the *cognoscenti* were taken in. One or two

Cue Frank!

BBC producers that Christmas sidled up and said, 'Tell me, did Eddie Waring *really* do a backward flip, two handsprings and a cartwheel or . . . well tell me, how the hell was it done!'

*   *   *   *   *

There was a different kind of chorus line for Bruce Forsyth's Christmas show. When *The Generation Game* was at the height of its popularity, anything could happen. I reported for duty to be disguised as Father Christmas along with the most bizarre collection of characters. The essence of the game was that the television theatre audience should under no circumstances see us before the recording began, so after rehearsals we were kicked out into Shepherd's Bush Green and told to get lost for a couple of hours. It was a Sunday afternoon and at that time Goldhawk Road, W12, is hardly humming – even the kebab shops are closed. We shambled along the pavement looking for a drink, a coffee, a sandwich – anything. I looked at my companions: disc jockey Tony Blackburn, wrestler Jackie Pallo, Bert Lynch from *Z Cars*, and Graham Stark, that excellent actor. It was unreal! All of us had been drawn together from different branches of the huge television business to dress up as Santa Claus, and were now rambling the streets at three o'clock on a Sunday afternoon.

We eventually reached the Lime Grove studios at the BBC, half a mile away from the theatre. There *Grandstand, Nationwide, Panorama, Tonight* – all the sport and current affairs programmes – are done, but at that time it seemed to be as dead as a dodo. However, small sounds were issuing from one of the small suites of hospitality rooms on the ground floor. We all trooped in politely. The occupants must have thought they were seeing things. They turned out to be the production team of one of the religious broadcasting programmes, who had just finished the final recording of the series and were having a glass of wine to mark the occasion. When they had recovered from their surprise, they offered us hospitality. One small unexpected cameo that followed I wouldn't have missed: Jackie Pallo and Tony Blackburn discussing the existence of Jesus Christ and the possibility of life after death!

On another occasion Cilla Black asked me to do a commentary on two teams of footballing dogs. I didn't like the idea too much, so I suggested to her that since I'd always wanted the opportunity to sing on television (the Oswestry choirs and eisteddfods wouldn't lie down!) why didn't she do the football commentary and I'd sing a song? The craziness of the idea appealed and the writer on the show produced for me a marvellous patter song to be sung to the tune of *The Entry of the Gladiators*. I enjoyed it immensely but sad to say the silence from Tin Pan Alley as a result was deafening!

8

UNACCUSTOMED AS I AM...

'Do you want to make your speech now, or shall we let them enjoy themselves a little longer?' The chairman of the dinner, resplendent in chain of office, meant well, but it was a gambit hardly designed to reassure me, as the last of the apple pie and cream was spooned away, and the hordes of waitresses descended on the top table with the coffee cups. They rattled like machine-gun fire, which to the speaker smacks of the firing squad, as he knows his moment is at hand. There is no hiding place, as the booze begins to bite, the cigars are lit, the chair-legs scrape round for a better view, and three hundred pairs of eyes focus, gimlet-like, upon you. Right, entertain us.

Actually, some of the most entertaining moments of all have come before I've even risen to speak. Although it was demoralising, albeit unwittingly, that chairman's remark at least had the great merit of being brief. Some of the introductions I've had as the guest speaker at a dinner have been longer than the speech. Give some people a microphone and they stay permanently erect, as if there's a stake down their backs preventing them from ever sitting down again. Mind you, the longer the introduction goes on, the more riveting I normally find it, because there's nothing more certain than that in the end, the speaker will fall headlong into a verbal pit of his, or her, own making.

The longest introduction I ever had – I usually time them, and this one ran for ten minutes – was delivered by the chairlady of a ladies' luncheon club in East Anglia. She had certainly done her homework. She began my biography at birth, went through my childhood, my adolescence, without a detail being omitted. Rarely, too, it was not only fluent but quite accurate. I was fascinated to see how long she could keep going. She reached my television days, and dealt in great depth with *Grandstand* and *Nationwide,* which was all very complimentary. Then, just when I thought she had established a new British all-comers' record for introductions, she came a hell of a cropper at the last hurdle. It was November and that year, 1976, we'd had a series of programmes on *Nationwide* called Citizen 76 in which we'd followed the pregnancies of five women, dealing with their hopes and fears, their problems, and their joy and excitement. In fact, we showed several of the babies being born, which, at 6.30 in the evening, prompted several letters demanding to know how we dared show such things while people were having their tea. The chairlady at last wound herself up to her grand finale. 'And finally, ladies', she said, 'I think we'd all like to say in welcoming Mr Bough amongst us, how well he has handled all those pregnant women'! Collapse of audience in total hysteria, while a very red-faced chairlady quickly sat down.

It is at moments like that, with the laughter ringing round the room, that I sometimes wonder how the hell I'm going to follow it. The delay in me getting to my feet has not always been because of the length of the introduction. I've known simple pieces of gear like gavels and microphones wreak such damage you wouldn't believe it. A Round Table chairman, young, determined to take his duties seriously, once enquired of me if I was ready to speak. Yes, I was. He rose to his feet and confronted the mass of boisterous, noisy, dinner-jacketed young men. Determined to get order, he crashed the gavel on the table in front of him with an almighty whack. At which point the supporting trestle at the end of the top table collapsed, and twenty officers and guests, pudding spoons in hands, leapt clear as plates, glasses, ashtrays, sugar bowls and flower arrangements cascaded past them, accelerating all the time as if down a ski-run!

In the Midlands on one occasion I rolled up improperly dressed. It was a very large assembly, and all were dinner-jacketed. Clearly the communications had broken down, because I had been convinced it was a lounge suit affair and I was wearing a very light grey one. I think the hosts were more embarrassed than I was. It didn't really matter to me, and there was nothing anyone could do about it anyway. (I have had that happen the other way round, though, with me resplendent in monkey suit while the rest of them, including Lord George Brown, the other guest speaker – and what a marvellous speech-maker the man is, too – in ordinary suits. That way it *can* be a bit of an inconvenience, because people are inclined to mistake you for the wine waiter!)

Cue Frank!

Anyway, with the coffee on the table, the preliminary speeches were started and a stand microphone about eighteen inches high was being passed up and down the top table for each speaker's use. Finally the chairman, on my right, called on the secretary, who was two seats down on my left, to introduce the guest speaker – me. The microphone was passed in front of me, the secretary reached over and lifted it towards him. Right in front of me was a bottle of red wine, almost full. It was like a slow motion replay. The microphone cable slowly wound its coil around the bottle, which tilted straight at me, and glug, glug, glug, half a pint of Mouton Cadet emptied itself, rich and red, on to the crotch of my pale grey suit. The poor lad was mortified. The fact that he had to make a speech was bad enough, he was really tense, and here he was, pouring red wine all over the guest.

To my rescue came the waitresses, who had clearly coped with such an emergency before. I was bundled backstage into the kitchen, told very firmly to remove my jacket, sit down, and stretch out my legs. I felt very vulnerable, with this dark stain spreading from my waist almost to my knees. As if by magic, sixteen salt cellars appeared and my private parts were bombarded as if being prepared for the cooking pot. What happened next was a male fantasy come true – female hands everywhere, patting and dabbing at my lap with cold, damp tea towels! It was much more fun being in the kitchen than in the dining room, I can tell you. Anyway, you may not be able to conjure up the females, but there is the perfect solution to wine stains for you. When my trousers were dry, only with the closest inspection could any mark be seen.

Let me tell you, if you ladies think that equality and emancipation are at hand, then you have a very long way still to go to achieve it! The great British stag dinner flourishes, there is no question of that. There are one or two rare female incursions, but they don't amount to much. For example, take the banks: there are five hundred dinner-jacketed managers at their Institute of Bankers dinner, and buried amongst them are possibly five ladies. Once I decided to give the chairman a dig. 'How are you coping with equal opportunity and all that?' 'Fine, fine, my boy – got a very open mind on that matter. Everybody's got a chance to rise to the top these days and the gals are doing splendidly. D'you know we have six assistant branch managers now who are ladies!' Big deal I thought, considering his bank has several thousand branches . . .

Mind you, the most remarkable piece of female emancipation I came across was in Luton at the annual dinner of the Luton and District Institute of Engineers, that most masculine of professions. The conversation I had before the dinner was with a lady whom I assumed to be the chairman's secretary. He ran his own light engineering firm. (So I *am* an MCP at heart!) I was astonished when I arrived to do my turn to find that the lady I'd been making the arrangements with was an engineer in her own right, the chairman of the Luton Institute, the only woman amongst the very large assembly. She was very glamorous, too.

In fact it is rather difficult to make a speech to an audience of, say, three hundred men and three or four women, yet that happens quite a lot these days. I am never deliberately crude when I make a speech, but there are some topics suitable for the chauvinistic bonhomie of a male gathering that are completely out of place when women are present. Yet believe it or not the speaker I remember getting the bird for being too blue, was speaking at an all-male dinner. That was in South Manchester, and he was a professional comic billed as 'the funniest man in Cheshire', a very modest billing I thought. Yet I sat open-mouthed as he committed professional suicide in front of two hundred men, all of whom, if he'd have toned down his language and his stories, could have ensured for him a long and financially happy career at other dinners in that area. They stamped and whistled him off the platform.

But stag still rules from north to south, of that there's no doubt. I once spoke in Preston, where the venue was a night club which had been taken over on a Monday night, and filled with men. An eerie, uncomfortable experience is a night club, with its soft furnishings and softer lighting, especially when full of monkey-suited men. It just didn't seem natural. I made my speech perched on a stool in the middle of a tiny dance floor, appearing between two strippers and a comic from Liverpool. Then again, in the poor suburbs of London, I appeared in one of those pubs with a hall attached. It was all very respectable, except that when the speeches were over, the chairman said, 'Well now, Frank, we have a small extra entertainment – I'm not sure what your particular style is in the matter, so if you want to go, we certainly won't feel offended'. After that, out of sheer curiosity, I couldn't go, could I? The 'extra entertainment' turned out to be a blue film show.

Cue Frank!

It was all very jolly, of course – and not very erotic when large assemblies of men are watching, because the remarks from the audience are usually vastly more entertaining than the action on the screen. When it was over, I said to my host, 'Tell me something. That's all very fine and dandy, but don't you ever worry that someone might drop in? After all, it's a respectable suburban area, there's the pub next door, people are passing all the time! If a curious policeman stuck his head around the door, there'd be an almighty scandal.' He regarded me with some condescension. 'Oh, no fear of that, none at all. It was the local CID who lent us the film in the first place.' Gulp.

These days, to go to a dinner without having to speak, to enjoy somebody else going through the hoop, is a real delight. That doesn't happen too often, and even when it does, I can never guarantee that I'm not going to get involved in the end. Reg Harris, that great cyclist who returned to the sport to win the British Championship again when he was over fifty, once invited me as a guest to an annual lunch at the Connaught Rooms – that vast suite of banqueting rooms, custom-built in all shapes and sizes, to accommodate what is known in the trade as the rubber chicken brigade. The occasion was the annual lunch of the Pickwickian Brigade Club – don't ask me what it was about, because I never really did discover why four hundred men all wore blazers and straw boaters, and recited stories of Bob Cratchit from Dickens, and toasted that great novelist after almost every forkful. It was delightful, but mystifying.

At the sherry session before the lunch I learned that the guest speaker was to be Blaster Bates, the demolition king, who has made a new career of telling hilarious stories about blowing things up, and occasionally people as well. He had been delayed, but the lunch would start without him. In we went, and sat down well away from the top table firing line at the bottom of the hall. I did notice that the guest speaker's chair alongside the chairman stayed empty throughout the soup, and then the fish. The meat came, and still there was no Blaster Bates. I can only imagine what the chairman was going through. Here was his big annual clambake, organised to the last button, with members and guests assembled from all over the British Isles, only the pudding was left and his cabaret was as yet nowhere in sight. My God, what a recipe for indigestion if you're lucky, heart failure if you're not.

Unaccustomed as I am . . .

Dishes clattered as the last of the *Poire Belle Hélène* was scraped away. At that point a flunkey appeared from a side door, sidled along the back of the top table and whispered in the chairman's ear.I couldn't hear what the chairman said but I lip-read enough to know that it wasn't very nice. Clearly Mr Bates was a non-starter.

The chairman stood up and set off. I knew where he was bound, I knew it. I buried my nose in my coffee and shrank. Along the top table, round the end, down the side he came, with a measured tread; along the back of the banqueting hall, and up to the table where I was sitting.

'Mr Bough, what can I say to you?'

'I know bloody well what you're going to say – he hasn't turned up, has he?'

'No.'

'Isn't going to, is he?'

'No.'

'You'd like me to make the speech?'

'If only you would . . . '

What can you do – the fellow's lunch is falling about his ears, he is living a nightmare. Tell you something, though. If the chairman introduces you as the guy who has agreed to stand in at five minutes notice because the invited speaker has failed to turn up, you can scratch your nose and they'll laugh, they're so relieved and grateful. They also gave me Blaster's cheque, which was nice!

9

NATIONWIDE AND BEYOND

An invitation to lunch from a member of the BBC hierarchy is an extremely worrying event, and those of us who are hired hands approach such occasions with great caution. It is a device the Corporation uses for a multitude of purposes; rather like Russian roulette, they could be inviting you to take up the post of Director General, or simply be giving you the bullet. 'Services no longer required. Thank you so much and goodbye. Another brandy, perhaps?'

I found myself mulling over such an invitation in February 1972. On the face of it, the unexpected missive seemed innocent enough. For a start it had come from a department for which I was not working at the time, current affairs, so the sack seemed unlikely – though not impossible. The BBC works in many devious ways. Secondly, the invitation had been issued by John Tisdall. If you're still with me, you'll remember that John was the news editor in Newcastle who had auditioned me and finally given me my first opportunity, the job of linking *Look North,* the regional news magazine programme, in 1962. He had risen in the world, had John, and he was now the deputy chief of the BBC's current affairs group.

Actually I looked forward to the occasion with some pleasure. I'd seen very little of John since those heady days in the north-east. We'd gone our various professional ways in the Corporation and, apart from the odd greeting, I'd seen little of him. The prospect of a leisurely lunch, accompanied no doubt by a reminiscence or two, was appealing. I couldn't help thinking that something was in the wind, if only because at fairly regular intervals over the previous ten years or so external events had tended to alter the course of my labours. I felt a proposition was brewing.

The West End restaurant John had chosen was certainly very different from the sawdust and brown ale of the old

Portland pub in Newcastle's New Bridge Street, where he'd offered me *Look North*. Mind you, to be absolutely honest, Notting Hill Gate is a little too far west to be strictly fashionable, but the restaurant was pleasant nevertheless.

We reviewed the progress of the Newcastle clan of 1962. It had certainly made its mark. The staff men had prospered. John had moved to London, and a senior post in the current affairs department; while Mike Alder, his assistant in the north-east, was now a very influential co-ordinator of the BBC regions' contribution to the television services output. The hire and fire merchants, like Harold Williamson and myself, had remained employed (and always be grateful for work in this life – it should be a treasured commodity) and had joined major network programmes – *Grandstand* in my case, *Man Alive* on BBC-2 in Harold's. Alex Glasgow, the Geordie composer-guitarist, was now something of a cult figure in the world of folk music. An hour can pass extremely pleasantly.

On occasions like this when something is afoot, the senses are sharpened by the excitement of some forthcoming revelation. The moment is not to be hurried, not to be precipitated by the anxious recipient. It is wise to look for clues as the conversation proceeds, but the imparter of the news will not be hurried. The denouement came with the coffee. 'Have you watched *Nationwide* recently?' asked John casually. Eureka!

At the time, early 1972, *Nationwide* had been careering its early-evening way across the screens of the nation, three days a week, for two-and-a-half years. On Tuesdays, Wednesdays and Thursdays, this brave, pioneering programme was attempting to reflect not only the national issues of the day, but also the richness and variety of life in non-metropolitan Britain. Unwittingly, it often made its own contribution to the scene. Drawing together the regional centres, and the outposts like Newcastle, Norwich, Southampton, and Plymouth, was an extremely hazardous technical adventure; so many and so catastrophic were the bloomers, often with hilarious consequences on air, that the programme had rapidly become compulsive viewing. But as Stuart Wilkinson, one of the programme's deputy editors, wrote in an admirable in-house guide to the programme and its production:

'Soon the audience watched for quite different reasons, and watched in increasing numbers. With its unique blend of hard-hitting reports, regional flavour and viewer involvement, *Nationwide* became part of the teatime routine in millions of households.

'For the first time, perhaps, BBC-1 had an early evening winner, a strong foundation upon which the network could be built, and it became simply a question of time before the three-night experiment blossomed into a five-night commitment. That step finally came in September 1972. With it came new opportunities and new responsibilities.'

John Tisdall poured me another cup of coffee. 'We're thinking of extending *Nationwide* from three nights a week to five this coming autumn. How do you fancy the idea of doing the extra two for us?'

Journalism is high amongst the most traditional of trades. Take any newspaper, and sport occupies the last four or five pages, with its headlines at the very back of the paper: firmly in its place. The rest of the paper contains daily news about 'life' – another subject entirely. It, too, appears firmly in its place. Though wrapped together in the same cover, rarely if ever do the two subjects meet. I was being invited to straddle that great divide. Standing for seven years, as I now have done, with my professional legs apart is not a comfortable position. I was interviewed recently on Downtown radio, Belfast's commercial station. Unwittingly, the disc jockey whose guest I was put it in a nutshell. Asking me about the problems of coping with two major programmes, *Grandstand* in sport and *Nationwide* in current affairs, he asked: 'Isn't it difficult, keeping both balls in the air at the same time?'

Actually it is. For instance, working for two bosses, each of whom is inclined to assume perfectly reasonably that your first loyalty is to him. Then there is the adjustment to be made, switching between two entirely different philosophies. The presentation of sport on the BBC is regarded as a crisp, factual, no-nonsense affair. Get on, give them the facts, and get off while they, the viewers, enjoy the event. Humour and frivolity is discouraged: sport is a deadly serious business. Only very recently has *Grandstand,* or our *Review of the Year* programme, allowed itself to parade deliberately the odd funny happenings from the year's programmes: such as commentators' blunders, and odd-ball recordings that never made the air. A year or two back, even to suggest such things was regarded as outrageous. It is strange really, because you'd expect the opposite – sport is supposed to be fun, after all, and to be entertaining.

Nationwide and Beyond

Perversely, *Nationwide,* which often reports on the awful consequences of man's inhumanity to man, is famous for its sense of fun. Presenters are encouraged to let their personalities emerge, to indulge themselves more than a little, to ad lib, to be themselves. In the early days of the programme, there is no doubt its fairly languid attitude to its presentation (which Sports Department would have regarded as so unprofessional), led to many of the on-air disasters that the audience at least found entertaining. On *Nationwide,* the sight of a cameraman trundling his camera in-vision behind an interview taking place would extract merely an 'oops-a-daisy' from the director. On *Grandstand* it would be a court-martial offence.

I pondered on all these matters during the early months of 1972. The problem that concerned me most was not the television side of *Nationwide.* So many years of live television in Sports Department, so much experience of linking complex international events, Olympic Games, World Cups, and *Grandstand* itself, had equipped me wonderfully for that side of it. Nor was I worried that I wouldn't be able to handle the programme's subject matter either. I am an avid reader and follower of news and current affairs anyway, and I had coped well enough in the smaller pool of *Look North* to reassure me that that would not be a great problem. No, what was worrying me was that viewers might not accept 'hard' news from me, that I was too firmly set in their minds as a practitioner of sports television. People are inclined to ask 'What on earth does he know about the falling pound? He's a sports commentator'. As I said, people are conditioned by newspapers; sport is over here, life is over there.

Right from the start, something told me I'd need the constitution of an ox to make it all succeed. You see, both disciplines are non-stop, week in, week out, throughout the whole year. I've often envied the series performers like Mike Parkinson, for example, who works his socks off for two-thirds of the year, say, and then his series has a break for several months, when he can recuperate, recharge his batteries, and do other things for a change. Sport and current affairs stride remorselessly on. For *Nationwide,* June and August are tick-over months, but only because, guess what, sport is dominating the airwaves. How on earth was I going to keep it up? Wouldn't it all be too much? Wouldn't viewers be sick of the sight of me anyway? The old bogey of over-exposure reared its head.

I met my new boss, *Nationwide* editor Michael Bunce. He was delighted that his programme had been extended from three nights to five, and was vastly enthusiastic about the programme's new future. He was looking forward to having me aboard.

'We're starting the new regime with a great bang', he said. 'We've lots of plans for the new season and it all begins in the first week of September, right after the Munich Olympic Games.'

I wilted at the thought of it. The 1968 Games had been the most demanding test of concentration and stamina ever devised to test the resolution of man, and I was to start my new programme the week after the 1972 Games finished. I knew now the state I would be in: one of absolute knackerment. It was about this time that news of my impending arrival reached the *Nationwide* team. One of them, I know, expressed the common thought openly. 'What on earth do we need a bloke from Sports Department for?' Old journalistic attitudes die hard!

You know how it is with a new job. You just wish like hell that you could start it six months in, so that you know what on earth is going on. During those summer months before I went to Munich for the Games, time and again I sat in the control gallery, watching the operation; studying the professional habits of the editor and the director; and watching during the office day how the programme content was put together. I picked up every crumb of information and knowledge that would help me in September when the time came for me to step aboard this great, speeding pantechnicon that had to produce an hour of television every weekday of its life.

Then I went to Munich, to be emotionally battered by the bewildering demands of an Olympic Games that ironically enough, perhaps, encapsulated both sport and news: the beauty of Ludmilla Tourescheva and the horrors of Middle East terrorism.

In 1972, *Nationwide*'s father figure was Michael Barratt, the Dimmock I'd followed into *Sportsview* and the Coleman I'd succeeded in the *Grandstand* chair. Michael was the archetypal new television journalist. He'd served a hard apprenticeship, reporting worldwide for *Panorama,* and now had an enormous enthusiasm for his new programme and the possibilities it presented. A domestic current affairs programme it might be, limited geographically to Britain in that sense, but as far as subject matter was concerned the boundaries were limitless. Michael is a Yorkshireman, gritty, gravel-voiced, with a strong dislike of fancy food. He was reared, I suspect, in Harry Ramsden's fish and chip emporium in the heart of the Holy Yorkshire Empire. His great ambition, it seemed to me, was to solve a national strike under the lights of the television studio. He never succeeded, but that never deterred him from making several brave efforts! Since its birth in 1969, he had been presenting the programme on all three nights – Tuesday, Wednesday and Thursday – and wanted to keep it that way. So I was to do the Monday and Friday programmes.

Still mentally jet-lagged from Munich, I marked my first appearance as the presenter of *Nationwide* by losing my cool completely. I work on a pretty slow fuse. That's the way I am made, and since live television requires all my energy, I like it that way. Tantrums and fits of temper are tiring, and I like to stay fresh. This, however, was a monumental row; I blew my top as never before.

I have to explain that *Nationwide* practice differs from *Grandstand* in many respects, but one of the most fundamental is that whereas the communications between the *Grandstand* gallery and my ear are total – 'omnibus talkback' we call it, in that I hear everything all the time – *Nationwide* uses 'switch talkback'. In other words, if instructions need to be communicated to me, like timings and changes of plan, a switch is pressed upstairs and the message is passed. Otherwise all is silence. In one sense, that is a good idea. If the programme is working well, and all is proceeding according to plan, then the presenter can concentrate on his work without being distracted by animated discussions of various people's problems in the gallery. On the other hand, since you cannot hear what is going on upstairs, you have no warning of impending disaster – and you have to rely on the switch being pressed and being told about it.

One of the items we had on this particular night was a piece about an old age pensioners' rally and march to the House of Commons, to lobby Members of Parliament for a better old age pension. We had film of the event, over which I was to describe what it was all about, followed by a live interview with two senior citizens in the Birmingham studio who had just got back to their native city after taking part in the rally. Up came the film nice and neatly, the words over fitted very well, and I then turned confidently to the monitor bank behind me, on to which was fed all the incoming circuits from the regions.

'In our Birmingham studio now are two of the marchers', I said. The screen was blank. A click came in my ear as talkback was switched on. '*Sorry, Frank, they're not there yet.*' I was furious. It seemed to me that if the pensioners were 'not there yet', they'd been 'not there yet' for a considerable time. Had I been warned, I could have eased my own and the programme's way out of the problem by saying simply that we were planning to talk to two of the marchers later on, or, indeed, by saying nothing at all and moving on to the next subject. Nobody would have had the slightest inkling that anything was wrong. As it was I looked a fool, but more importantly the programme looked inefficient, and that really upset me. After the programme I really raved about how unnecessarily stupid we had all been made to look, and demanded omnibus talkback in my ear. If they were not prepared to let me in on the problems, I would at least be able to overhear them myself, however distracting that might be.

The fact is though, that eight years of effort later the programme has become very professional indeed. It has been hammered and coaxed into shape by four editors in that time. I never worked under Derrick Amoore, the editor who had the daunting job of launching the great *Nationwide* machine into orbit, but Michael Bunce, who first hired me, John Gau, who followed him, and the current boss, Hugh Williams, have all picked up the challenge and brought new ideas to the presentation and content.

The remarkable quality that *Nationwide* has is that it is as much a family programme behind the camera as it is on screen. I don't want to be maudlin about it, but it is extraordinary that through all the changes of leadership, everyone has got on so well together; especially when you bear in mind that every day, come five to six, a full hour of topical and entertaining television has to have been invented, treated, planned, and made ready for transmission.

Of course, there is aggravation from time to time, as there is in the best ordered family units, but given the pressures, the spirit and togetherness has never really wavered. I'm talking about the central team of thirty or so people, living in each other's pockets day after day. It is not really for me to say, but we like to think that we are a caring programme on air, both to our guests and to our audience, who write to us like family friends. They chastise us, they encourage us, and somehow are part of the whole family themselves.

There has always been a great deal of thoughtfulness and mutual consideration in the office and studios, too. I've known it happen that at 5.30pm or so – with only twenty-five minutes to go until transmission time and everybody furiously beavering away to put the final touches to a very complicated series of programme items – all activity has stopped and a little speech and presentation made to a departing colleague, or someone who has just got married, or someone who is to have a baby, because that was the right time to do it, and doing it was very important. I marvelled the first time that happened; it still happens now, and I hope it never stops. I like to think that such an attitude of good comradeship comes through the glass when we present the programme. Certainly we could never feign the fun we sometimes have if we were constantly back-biting in the office.

An ever-ready helping hand is always there in the studio, too, from presenter to presenter. We are all prepared to live, with the odd blunder, since I'm convinced the audience enjoys them. The occasional disaster does remind people that we are there for real, live, and are not just programmed to total efficiency by some remote BBC computer. With so many recorded programmes these days, with all the boobs edited out, a live programme like *Nationwide* or *Grandstand* is a relatively rare animal.

There have been some real disasters, too. One evening, my final job was to introduce the very last item on the pro- gramme, which was a five-minute report on progress in the *Nationwide* allotment in Birmingham. Because it was winter, the item had been recorded on videotape earlier in the afternoon while it was still light.

As my words set up the piece and explained that this week we were going to find out how the cabbages were doing, I waited for the run-cue in my ear and the ten-second count into the recording. It never came. All was silence. I waffled a bit, spreading the words out, but still nothing happened. Some- body pressed the talkback switch and said in my ear: *'We can't find it. Hang on.'* I waffled some more. Next instruction: *'We haven't got it. Lines from Birmingham have gone!'*

Now ninety-nine times out of every hundred we have a

standby item ready and waiting for such an emergency. It may be that a guest fails to turn up, or a film cannot be put together in time for the programme. We always have something to fall back on. Quite often, after all, we have to change our plans on air, which is the very essence of a live, up-to-date, current affairs programme.

Another check. *'Sorry, Frank. We haven't got the allotment report and we haven't got anything else either. Four-and-a-half minutes to the end of the programme.'*

Now *Nationwide,* just like *Grandstand,* ends on the clock, right on time. We never overrun, nor do we finish early. The whole planning of a BBC-1 network evening, with regions joining and leaving, is locked into the clock. Four-and-a-half minutes may not seem a very long time, but you try, starting now without warning, to talk intelligently and interestingly for four-and-a-half minutes. It feels like a lifetime.

'Sorry, we aren't going to get our report from Birmingham' I said, smiling bravely into the camera. 'But I tell you something, my own cabbages are doing just fine. I'm feeding them a mixture of this and that, and the hearts are hardening up quite nicely.' My mind raced around my own little garden plot, trying desperately to remember what we had sown, and how it was doing. I eventually ran out of vegetables.

'Three minutes to the end of the programme.' My God, what next? The funny thing was that Sue Lawley and Bob Wellings, who had been doing the programme with me, had long since left the studio. Their own jobs were finished and they had left me to run the Birmingham tape and close the programme on my own. Seeing my dilemma, they set off from various parts of the seven-floor building to rush back to my aid. Bob never made it. He pressed the wrong lift button and zoomed past the studio floor level, never to return: very Bob-like!

Sue did make it. She raced in, and sat down in a chair alongside me, off camera, ready to help. I turned to her gratefully. She immediately started prattling on about the cow we had shown on the programme a little earlier, forgetting that it had been an item in the south-east part of the programme so seventy-five per cent of the audience hadn't seen it, and must have thought she had gone off her head!

'Two minutes to the end of the programme.' Nightmare! I suddenly decided that instead of trying to cover up any further, a touch of honesty was by far the best solution. I

remembered seeing Mike Neville, who now presents the *Look North* part of *Nationwide* up in my old Newcastle studio, coping wonderfully with such a breakdown. The production team had got their timings a little wrong, and he had been left to fill two minutes of air time until network *Nationwide* drew everybody together at 6.20pm.

'They've left me stranded' he began, in that beautiful Geordie accent of his, 'the people who run this outfit. Don't go away, will you? We'll be joining *Nationwide* in a minute or two.'

He then put his feet up on the presenter's desk, picked up that morning's copy of the *Northern Echo* and proceeded to read it, punctuating the silence with an odd 'See the weather forecast's not so good.' 'What are Newcastle doing about their football team?' 'Are you still there?' 'Won't be half a minute.' Were they still there! They loved it – and Mike was obviously in his element when things were going wrong!

So I decided to follow his example, and come clean. 'You think I'm in complete control of this crisis, don't you?' I said. 'Well, I'm not. We've nothing left and there's two minutes to go. What would you do' I asked, 'given two minutes of peak hour television time?' I staggered through it somehow. Later that week Radio 4 played the whole of my gobbledegook on their *Pick of the Week* programme. It must have made hypnotic listening!

* * * * *

The joy of *Nationwide* is that the subject matter we can tackle is absolutely unlimited. We are there to reflect life in Great Britain, a life which is extraordinarily varied, and therefore the programme should cover immensely weighty matters alongside lighthearted ones. The task of the programme editor is to blend together the right mixture to inform and entertain for an hour each evening. Great weight is placed on giving the programme the right 'mix', as we call it, and on the arrangement of the items, be they films or interviews or demonstrations or whatever, in the appropriate order.

You must also remember that the time we appear, in the early part of the evening, is a very busy time of day for a great many people. True, there are those who do live pretty near to their work, and can be home, fed and seated in a chair by six or so; but many are only just arriving home, saying hello to the children, preparing meals, feeding babies. The format of

Cue Frank!

Nationwide is such that you can pause for a minute or two to watch an item that interests you, or catches your attention, and then return to what you are doing. Ours is not necessarily a time of day when people are ready to sit and give their undivided attention to an in-depth conversation on the economic state of the nation, or the latest industrial crisis. We do, when the occasion demands it, devote the whole programme to one subject, but the magazine style, with twelve or thirteen items over the hour, is unbeatable at that time of the evening.

Mind you, we are always complaining that the editor of the day never gives us enough time for an interview. 'What? Only three minutes to talk about the budget proposals that the Chancellor spent three hours over in the Commons today?' is an oft-heard complaint from a presenter!

The joy of the programme is in discovering what a variety and richness of life there is in this country. I've never understood those professional television critics who dismiss *Nationwide* out of hand as being frivolous. Certainly, being frivolous and amusing is an important part of the programme. We make no apologies for that, because, thank God, there is so much light-heartedness about; and we are there, I repeat, to reflect British life, which we find is far from gloomy and introspective. Over the years, *Nationwide* viewers have been charmed to discover that the real reason that Al Jolson beat his knees while he sang was because it gave him relief from his ingrowing toenails; and what about the man who built himself a fifty-six-ton concrete boat at Benfleet creek in the Thames estuary, where the water level was four inches! Then there was Mrs Dorothy Arnold, who in her will left her favourite aspidistra to the great plant gardeners at Syon Park, because she couldn't be sure that if she died before her husband, he would give it all the love to which it had grown accustomed. We spoke to Mrs Olive Haynes of Birmingham, who'd attended ten thousand weddings in thirty-three years; to Councillor John Smith of Brighton, who was so utterly entertaining at council meetings that he had been offered a one-night stand in a local night club. We told the story of the Watt family from Brasted in Kent, who were all butchers: grandad, father, and eight-year-old Eric. There was that football team from Oxfam Social Club, Wolverhampton, who had gone on a continental tour, mixed their fixtures up, and somehow played SVW Mainz – losing 21-0! And what about the Alderson sisters, Dorothy Mary and Elizabeth Margaret?

Both were dedicated painters of horses and other animals; they lived in the same farmhouse they were born in, and worked together on the same canvas. Dorothy Mary would start with the head of the horse and Elizabeth Margaret at the tail, and the pair of them hoped to meet somewhere in the middle!

We have heard a visiting Japanese rugby team singing *My bonny lies over the ocean*; visited a school for night club bouncers; commiserated with Mrs Mitsa Panayiotone who sent off a pools coupon that would have won her £500,000, had Littlewoods ever received it; we've been to the World Champion Gooseberry Show, the National Conker Championships, and the National Stilt Walking Championships.

Frivolous? Well, if being popular and entertaining is being frivolous, I suppose so. But such things go on, all over Britain. Why should we ignore them, for heaven's sake? The curious thing is, the critics never seem to be watching when we are tackling the serious matters of life, or are showing concern over some injustice, which we do every evening. They didn't see our regular programmes on the state of the nation in 1979, or on cancer in the same year. They missed our coverage of the thalidomide tragedy, our 'cause for concern' series, our commitment to consumers, budgets, general elections, day-to-day politics. Every prime minister and leader of the opposition, as well as the leading cabinet ministers, trades union leaders and industrialists, have been put 'on the spot'. We maintain that our reflection of life is comprehensive; and why British current affairs should need to be presented in a dull and worthy manner, is beyond me. There is a lot of fun around and *Nationwide* is in the business of reporting it.

For my part, the most challenging and difficult work we do on *Nationwide* are the interviews. I have already said that we all argue for a little more time in which to do them, largely because with a little more time, we have a better chance of making them tell. These interviews are almost invariably done live, unless we have to record during the afternoon because our guest can't make it during transmission time. To conduct an interview successfully – and by that I mean one that is balanced, has a beginning, a middle and an end – in three or four minutes is a very elusive affair. The interviewee may well be very nervous. Possibly it is his or her first and last time in a television studio; or on the other hand, the guest may be a very experienced and regular television performer, like a politician, and that presents difficulties of a different kind. Let me explain what I mean, so that the next time you see a politician being interviewed you'll know what to look out for.

Let us assume a backbench MP has been lucky in the draw and has the opportunity to launch a Private Member's Bill in the House of Commons. He is invited to discuss it on *Nationwide* and accepts. The odds are, if he has thought it worth the trouble, he has been to one of several television training schools that exist to help politicians, businessmen, trade unionists, and members of the armed services, to conduct themselves properly when they are being quizzed on the box: what to wear, how to sit, and most important of all, how to marshal their arguments. So our MP will sit down, perhaps with his agent, and work out tactics.

'Now *Nationwide,* four minutes interview if I'm lucky, three more likely than not! So I must make sure I get in all I want to say. First and most important I must stress the benefits my Bill will bring – that's point A. Then there are the spin-offs – the people who will gain from it by implication – that's point B.' And his agent will say 'And you mustn't forget to stress the local benefits the Bill will bring. That'll go down very well in the constituency and might win us a few more votes in the next election. Make that point C.' And so on, and so on.

It is worth remembering if you ever have the opportunity of being interviewed on television, and thousands do these days, to ask all the relevant questions about what is going on: where the cameras are that matter, where you look, what the line of questioning is likely to be. You have obviously got some idea about that, because you have already been approached and invited on the programme, and there is always a reason. I have known an MP to ask 'Which is my camera, the one that's pointing at me?' 'Over there', I've said, 'camera four'. 'Ah, that's my wrong side', he said. 'My wife tells me I look much more presentable from the other side.' Always happy to please, we changed sides!

So in our MP comes, has a pat or two of make-up to take the shine off his nose, and the interview begins.

'Tell me about your Bill', I say, 'because one of the criticisms being levelled at it is that it's far too limited in its objectives'.

'Ah well, you see', he replied, 'What you must remember is that Rome wasn't built in a day and what is important about it is that . . .' And bang, in goes point A!

I press him a little further. 'But what I mean by limited in its objectives is that it completely ignores the particular problems of the whole of the north-west of England.'

'Ah yes, it is our intention to tackle that later, but on the other hand . . .' and bang, in goes point B!

And so on, through the interview, each question being neatly turned and room made for exactly the answers the interviewee wants to give, and the points he wants to drive home. No wonder Robin Day sits patiently and asks the same questions three or four times, until he gets a proper and not an evasive answer!

Allow me to let you into another secret, if only because it may help to deflect complaints we sometimes get from viewers that we rudely interrupt our guests, cutting them off and ending the interview abruptly. I have already explained that the programme has to finish on time, to the second. Of course, if you think about it, we have another fixed point to meet, all of us, and I include all the presenters in the regional studios and in Wales, Scotland, and Northern Ireland, at 6.20pm. That is the time, precisely the time – not a second earlier, not a second later – that the engineers push in the plug that ends the first part of *Nationwide,* in which all the regions talk to their own audience, and brings us all together in one net-worked programme.

The ingredients of those first twenty minutes are all very carefully timed: the length of the films, of which there may be two or three, the length of the news content, and the length of the links between items. Whatever minutes remain are live interview time. Everything has to add up to exactly twenty minutes.

Thus if the final item is an interview, lasting say three minutes, it has to end on the clock, however far you have managed to get, or whoever is in full flow when the time is up. Throughout – and the same thing is happening in Belfast, Bristol, Cardiff, Glasgow, Manchester, Birmingham, Plymouth, and the rest – the producer's assistant in the control gallery is telling the interviewer in his ear how long there is to go. '*Three minutes to the opt.*' (The opt is 6.20pm when all the regions 'opt back' to the network.) '*Two minutes to the opt.*' The interview is proceeding. '*One minute to the opt.*' The presenter is trying to put his 'round-off' question. '*Thirty seconds to the opt.*' The interviewee is in full flow.

With twenty seconds to go, the interviewer has a difficult

choice. He or she can either play safe, by thanking the interviewee there and then in lengthy and effusive style, and hand over to Sue or me in an extravagant fashion, all of which is wasteful of good television time. Or, and this is living dangerously, throw in a final question in the hope that the reply will be short and concise. That is usually the moment when the guest, who is naturally unaware of how little time is left (by now only fifteen seconds or so), says 'Well, there are four things I'd like to say in answer to that'! There is no way he can say them I'm afraid, and that's when the viewers get cross because the interviewer has to dive in and bring the discussion to a very rapid conclusion. However well it is done, of course, it always looks discourteous.

* * * * *

Many of our guests are public figures: politicians, trades union leaders, businessmen, most of whom are very much at home in a television studio. It can be a rather intimidating place, if you are appearing on *Nationwide* for the first time. We have many guests who that day are news, because they have done something brave, or stupid, or ridiculous, or they have won the pools, perhaps. For them, television belongs in that box in their lounge; and when for some reason they find themselves inside the box, even those who are normally intelligent and self-assured can go to pieces. There is really no knowing how people will behave under the stress of a live interview. That's just another of the charms and hazards!

One evening I had the job of interviewing two such people. She was a quiet, nervous, elderly lady, in the news for a day. He had never been inside a television studio either, but was articulate, self-assured, and very confident.

It was 5.45pm, all hell was on in the studio, with instructions being shouted, adjustments being made to a set over in what we call our demonstration area, cameras being trundled here and there, and cables everywhere.

We like to look after our guests, to reassure them, and let them know what is going on. I started with the lady.

'Hello, dear, everything all right?' I began brightly.

'Mm' – little weak smile.

'Don't worry about all this noise and activity. It'll be quiet when the programme starts. All you have to do is try and ignore everything and everybody and when we talk on the programme, just let's talk together as if we were at home.'

'Mm' – gulp.

'Tell you what, let's have a little practice', I said encouragingly. 'What I'll do, I'll start by asking you how your special day began this morning.' Silence. 'What will you say when I ask you that?'

'You mean this morning?' she spoke.

'Yes.'

'Well . . . er – er.'

'Now don't worry about a thing, just tell me in your own words what has happened today. I'll nudge you along a little to remind you, don't worry about a thing. Glass of water?'

'Yes, please.'

She was really nervous. My heart sank, because we'd planned several minutes for her. It was going to be hard work. 'Never mind, dear, try and relax, all will be fine.' I wish I was as confident as I sounded.

I thought I'd better have a chat to the gentleman. It was now five minutes before transmission.

'Now, sir, I thought I'd start by asking you . . . '

He cut me short. 'You just fire away, Frank old son, don't bother about me. I'm really going to tell 'em! I've never been more furious about something in my whole life.'

My spirits lifted. Here was a man who was going to be no trouble, and who looked like being very positive and entertaining as well.

We're on the air. I smiled reassuringly at the little old lady, still trying to decide as the programme titles were running what to do to coax her into a few words. A few seconds later we're on. I introduced her.

'Tell me, how did this wonderful day begin for you?'

She spoke clearly, proudly, and very movingly, about her big day. I marvelled. She was terrific.

'And what happened then?' A nudge here, a reminder there, and the nervous old lady was a thing of the past. The light was on, she was on air, and had risen to the occasion wonderfully.

I was well pleased – particularly since on my other side was a self-confident, strong interviewee I knew was going to be easy. I thanked the lady, turned to him and introduced him, explained why he was there, and threw the first question at him.

'Tell me, what is it about all this that has made you so cross?' Then I relaxed. I shouldn't have done.

'What you mean – er –.'

Cue Frank!

He had blown it. He had seen the lights come on and hadn't a thought in his head. The interview dropped straight through the floor! There's just no telling.

Funnily enough, I've never found interviewing the famous at all intimidating. That may sound pretty arrogant. But I'm sure that if you are at all keen to make a competent job of it, there is so much to cope with, and so many professional disciplines bearing down on you, that there is no time to be overcome by the interviewee's grandness. I do suffer from the old dry mouth occasionally, when no amount of sips of water will prevent my lips gumming together like bluetack, but that has always been because of a desire to make the very best of an opportunity rarely offered.

For example, you don't get a prime minister through your hands very often, so if you *are* given an opportunity the adrenalin does tend to rush through the system a little quicker. Even so, I have recognised in all the four prime ministers I've interviewed their own particular method of screwing themselves up to the sticking point, so as to present the best sides of both their politics and their personalities. We all need to reassure ourselves, to polish our confidence, when we are faced with a public examination.

In 1974 I was charged with the job of quizzing Harold Wilson, at the time of the big debate on our membership of the Common Market. The country was to vote by a referendum on whether Britain should remain a member. Mr Wilson let it be known that he would like to inject a note of enthusiasm into the campaign at the beginning of the week in which polling was to take place. It certainly needed it. Important issue though the Common Market was, it didn't seem to rouse the nation to ecstatic interest, and after three weeks of public debate the sound of apathy was deafening.

The interview was to take place on *Nationwide* on a Monday evening. I spent the whole of Sunday doing my homework, blocking out the various subjects I wanted to deal with, and revising my own knowledge of the issue, particularly the aspects that seemed to be worrying the voters most. These had been thrashed to death for days, and I worked hard at trying to add some freshness to arguments about the agricultural policy, threats to our independence as a major parliamentary democracy, wine lakes, butter mountains and the sovereignty of our royal family.

I have a feeling that the prime minister did his homework

too. After all, a television appearance is always a great opportunity for a politician to make his point, and is therefore to be approached with diligence.

Even the selection of *Nationwide* must have been given thought. After all, he could have had *Panorama,* which also goes out on Monday night. 'Highly prestigious, prime minister' he would have been advised, 'but too rarefied for the general public, and not a very large viewing audience'. I've no doubt *24 Hours,* the BBC's late evening current affairs programme at that time, was also discussed. 'Well, prime minister', his PR guy would have said, 'always the danger that they're still in the pub or gone to the pictures'. *Nationwide*? 'Well, prime minister, the interviews on *Nationwide* tend to be short, but because you are prime minister, and television producers like to have prime ministers on their programmes, I'm sure that you'll be given plenty of time, say fifteen minutes or so.' If that is how the argument went, they were right. We do, and he was given plenty of time.

Prime ministers travel about, as you probably know, surrounded by a small court of advisers, both political and social, including the inevitable press attaché, the public relations officer. When his or her little caravan comes to rest in the Lime Grove studios of the BBC, the numbers are swollen by not only the editor, producer and presenter of the *Nationwide* programme, but also the Controller of the channel, in this case BBC-1, and even the Director General, who feels, and rightly, that a prime minister should be accorded a rather extra politeness or two and a warm welcome. All this, in a BBC hospitality room, makes it very difficult for the poor interviewer, who only wants to take his subject aside, and establish a little rapport at least to help build a relationship which will in the end make for a better interview on the air. At last, when all the welcoming formalities and greetings are over and it is time to go to work, the bosses and administrators have to withdraw and leave the interviewer to his work bench, that little desk set in the *Nationwide* studio.

We sat alone now, waiting to begin. The famous pipe was ignited and burning well. A minute before we began, he performed what I'm convinced was a recognisable, professional, confidence-boosting routine.

'Tell me', he said, 'you get quite a good audience for this *Nationwide* programme, don't you? How many viewers do you reckon?'

Cue Frank!

'Well, prime minister', I said. 'You're right, it's a very high audience indeed for this time of the evening. At most times of the year, it's rarely below eight million, and in the depths of winter, when people like to stay in, very often up to eleven million.'

He removed the pipe, looked sideways at me, and delivered the *coup de grâce*. 'Good' he said. 'They are my kind of people, you know.' Whack! As much as to say, 'I know you've got to sit there and move me along from time to time, but don't get in the way boy – I'm here to talk to the people!' Bough was put in his place very firmly. Actually, he had given me just the little prick I needed to put me on my mettle. Far from intimidating me, his attitude made me square my shoulders and pitch in.

I remembered afterwards a boxer called Frankie Taylor. I was doing a radio programme with him about the loneliest places in sport; the boxing ring is certainly one of those. 'It's funny' he said. 'When the fight is going against me, I always hear the bookies at the ringside lengthening the odds against me. Bugger them, I tell myself, and find new strength I never knew I had!' I know what he meant.

When Jim Callaghan was prime minister, I interviewed him at Number 10, which gave me an opportunity of looking inside that lovely house. It really is a piece of British history in itself, 10 Downing Street, with reminders everywhere of the prime ministers who have served the country over so many years and of the great events that have taken place.

'Sunny' Jim was just that. Exuding bonhomie and charm, he made me feel very much at ease, and replied to questions in that confidential, matter of fact style of his. At one point he said 'Look, I haven't told anybody else this yet', and my heart warmed to him, imagining that we were about to get a really exclusive scoop. On reflection, when we listened to the interview, we decided he had fed me some fairly inconsequential crumb of information that wasn't that special at all! Nevertheless, it made one feel very good. A kind man, I thought.

Margaret Thatcher's approach is very different – aggressive replies, flinty, and she has a habit of throwing questions at the interviewer, which isn't in the rules at all. My stock defence against that gambit is to say 'Well, prime minister, nobody has the slightest interest in what *I* think of the matter' and plough on! I have found her an exciting person to interview, because of her positive, no-nonsense approach, which after all is a very large part of her appeal as a leader.

Nevertheless, she has left one or two interviewers in her wake severely mauled and licking their wounds.

Of all the great and successful men and women I've interviewed and admired, and perhaps even envied just a little, the one who undoubtedly carries the greatest burden of all is Prince Charles. For all his royal palaces, his entourage, and his status as a highly regarded heir to the throne, he has less freedom than any of us. The rules of his particular game are very rigid indeed, and although he has influence, backed by great affection and goodwill from the country, he has to achieve his aspirations within very limited confines.

An interview with the next King of England is a very rare plum indeed for any broadcaster. Yet I have had both to encourage him to speak, and on another occasion to persuade him to stop while in full verbal flow.

The opportunity of an interview came in the Queen's Jubilee year – 1977. The Prince of Wales took it upon himself to mastermind the success of the Jubilee, and in particular to encourage the fund-raising for the various causes that were to benefit from it. His particular enthusiasm was for encouraging the young people of Great Britain to get off their backsides and do something useful – something that they could enjoy, but which at the same time would be of service to less fortunate members of the community, particularly the old and the handicapped.

Like every good idea that involves the participation of millions of people, it needed good, old-fashioned advertising and promotion. *Nationwide* decided it could help, since five nights a week millions of the kind of people that the Prince wanted to get through to watched the programme.

After long discussion with Prince Charles's Youth Committee, Gordon Watts, the producer in charge of *Nationwide*'s efforts in the matter, agreed that we would select half a dozen of the Prince's favourite projects and feature them in a series of films to be shown in the programme. I know Gordon had a long, slogging time of it, dealing with people who had their own pet projects which they thought were more important than anyone else's. Some of them, though worthy, were dreadfully dull, and Gordon sought to fix on the ones that were more entertaining from a television point of view. His other objective, apart from making the films, was to persuade Prince Charles that he should make a personal appearance on *Nationwide* to launch the series. Frankly, he would be wonderful box office, but also the programme could give him a stage from which he could communicate his Jubilee idea to a very large audience.

Well, everybody appears on television these days, and you would have thought that that was a very reasonable request. From the Jubilee Youth Appeal's point of view, it was a very desirable one too, to give the scheme a real push. But it proved to be a very difficult nut to crack, even given the goodwill of everybody, including the Prince himself.

I was to be the presenter of the proposed programme. The idea was that I would first interview Prince Charles, and then chair a studio question and answer session, during which the Prince would have points fired at him by a studio audience of young people, the sort of youngsters who were engaged in the community projects he was anxious to encourage. As I attended the committee meetings with Gordon, it began to dawn on me what a pig of a job Prince Charles has.

The stumbling block was that he had never before been exposed to a live studio audience. He had been interviewed, he had made films, but never before had he been put on the spot as it were. Never before had he been made so dangerously accessible – even to the obviously sympathetic questioning we had in mind!

As Prince Charles is prepared for the day when he will be King Charles III, there is a continuous process going on to lay down the ground rules of his reign. For Her Majesty The Queen, born and brought up in another generation, those rules have long since been fixed and are rock-hard. Nobody is going to invite Queen Elizabeth II to be interviewed on *Nationwide*. Nobody will be allowed to stick a microphone under her nose at Badminton to ask her how the corgis are, let alone quiz her on more important matters. The Queen's ground rules are set. But Prince Charles is of another, easier, more accessible age. He has already made himself public property, he is approachable, he lives, as far as an heir to the throne can without devaluing the aura and magic of the monarchy, amongst his people. But as the demands on him grow, and the media want more and more of him, he and his advisers have to decide how far to go and when to draw the line.

In the case of our interview, we were proposing something quite new. If our request was granted, and a new access agreed, it would have to be allowed in future. A precedent would be built into the rules, so that the same facility could be granted to other television organisations.

His Royal Highness was inclined to say yes. Obviously the publicity given to the Youth Appeal would be considerable, and that attracted him. But before making up his mind, he wanted to consult directly with the people involved, cutting out the intermediaries who had been dealing with the matter so far.

Gordon and I went to the Palace. In his study, the Prince poured us drinks, and we set about reassuring him that everyone involved, including the youngsters we were inviting to the studio, was on his side. He smiled somewhat wryly. 'I don't doubt your good intentions at all', he said, 'but in the end, all anybody wants to ask me is when I'm getting married and to whom'! However, to our delight, he agreed to the whole proposal. Then we tackled the subject of dress. A funny subject, you might think, and rather presumptuous of us to try and guide the Prince of Wales on what to wear and when. He, of all people, must have an acute awareness of what is appropriate on all occasions. The only point we wanted to make was that the youngsters in the studio would be in their usual daily kit – denim jeans, sweat shirts, long hair – youth *à la mode* as it were. Therefore we wanted him to know that it was to be an extremely informal affair.

At that point, our courage failed us, but he got us off the hook. 'Thank you', he said. 'I appreciate your concern and I'm glad of the information. But we never can win you know. Let's take as an example a royal tour of an African state. If the Queen doesn't step off the aeroplane in a long gown with the crown on her head and the orb and sceptre in each hand, there are those who don't believe she is the Queen, because that's what she's always wearing in the picture on the wall!'

In the end, he rolled up immaculately clad in a suit, shoes highly polished and knife-edge creases in his trousers. He answered the questions from the youngsters admirably. At a later date, he also produced a highly efficient piece of filming from one of the projects, with himself as the reporter; it is as though he relishes enormously having a go at the things most of us do for a living, but then he has to retire, rather reluctantly, to the job he was born to do.

In the following year, 1978, it was my misfortune to have to cut Prince Charles off in full flow. He had accepted an invitation to be our guest of honour at the BBC's *Sports*

Cue Frank!

Review of the Year programme in early December. We pick the highlights out of a year of televised sport, and then, in front of an audience of considerable quality – world champions, gold medallists, title holders, administrators and others – the Sports Personality of the Year Trophy is presented to the sportsman or woman voted by the viewers as their particular favourite. His Royal Highness was to make the presentation, and say a few words to the winner, the audience, and the fifteen million viewers at home.

Unfortunately, our biggest coup in getting Prince Charles coincided with a spot of industrial action at the BBC. The lads were working to rule, which meant that programmes had to finish precisely at the time they were billed to finish in *Radio Times*. There could be no over-running. Well, *Sports Review of the Year* always over-runs, perhaps only by a minute or two; nobody worries too much about it because it is live, the length of applause is impossible to estimate, and nobody is quite sure how long the distinguished speaker is going to perform for either.

This year we *had* to be off on time, otherwise the programme would be faded off the air, and that meant almost certainly when Prince Charles was doing his bit right at the very end of the programme. We worked like beavers to ensure that there would be plenty of time left so that the unthinkable wouldn't happen. Throughout we were smack on course, but there was always the one unknown factor – the length of Prince Charles's speech.

The climax of the programme arrived. There was great applause as I announced that His Royal Highness, Prince Charles, would now announce the result of the viewers' poll for the Sports Personality of the Year. He went through the top three in reverse order, just like Miss World. The winner was that great athlete, Steve Ovett. Prolonged applause . . . it was all very exciting, but too prolonged . . . time was passing, passing.

Prince Charles, trophy in hand, and Ovett occupied centre stage. My job in the programme was by now virtually finished. As soon as the prize was handed over all I had to do was to say an out of vision farewell into a microphone off-stage, as the credits ran and the end music played. Prince Charles started his speech. In my ear piece I could hear the control room was in a state of panic. There was now so little time left that there was a very real chance that we would become the first programme in the history of television to put a member of the royal family off the air while in full flow.

Jonathan Martin, the editor of the programme, was leaping around at the back of the control room like a demented grasshopper. 'What can we do? What *can* we do?' Somewhere in the system was an engineer, with a rule book in one hand, and the other on a switch, preparing to do the unthinkable. Penny Wood was reeling off the time left: 'One minute to cueing titles.' Prince Charles warmed to his task. His speech was going down well, to more applause. 'Thirty seconds to cueing titles' said Penny.

'Frank', said Jonathan. 'You've got to get back in there and interrupt him, before he gets faded out.'

I went pale. How do you interrupt the next King of England while he is talking to fifteen million of his loyal, adoring subjects? I waltzed breezily back to centre stage, wondering briefly what life was really like in the Tower of London . . .!

'Fifteen seconds to cueing titles' howled Penny Wood. 'We must be out on time.'

Either the man has extra-sensory perception, or he is simply a terrific professional, but at that moment Prince Charles stopped talking and to tumultuous applause handed the trophy to Ovett. I could have hugged him. I was in like a rapier.

'Your Royal Highness, it's a great honour you've done us being here tonight. Thank you so much for making our presentation. To Steve Ovett, our warmest congratulations and to you all at home a very good night.'

It was the most abrupt, sharp end to the programme we'd ever had, but we had got away with it. I just stood there and trembled.

Mind you, there was one review of the year presentation speech that had us really up a gum tree. Our guest of honour was Colonel Sir Mike Ansell of the British Show Jumping Association. You will have seen him, I'm sure, being led round the arena at the Royal International and Horse of the Year Shows at Wembley, because despite being completely blind, Colonel Mike is the organising genius behind those very complex operations. For several years I introduced those two events, the job that David Vine does so admirably now. To attend the morning meeting each day of the show, when Colonel Mike briefed the team that was helping him, was a revelation. Despite his handicap, nothing escaped him, no detail that might upset the smooth running of the show was allowed to go unattended, from the catering to the flowers, the guests, the state of the course, or the music. Ken Griffin, who was then responsible for the music and the band, and now a BBC producer, used to complain that he of all people could never escape the Colonel's wrath, because although the old man couldn't see anything, his ears were firmly tuned to pick out a wrong note or a late music cue. He ran those meetings with military precision. It was quite uncanny to watch him in action.

Well, he accepted our invitation to be our special guest of honour at *Sports Review of the Year*. He was briefed, and had the layout of the stage described to him. (He liked to visualise every scene, and would have it described in great detail.) Would he say a few words, please, and then present the trophy.

Would he say a few words! My God, he launched into his speech with great verve, and it soon became apparent that Colonel Mike was going to make the most of his opportunity.

Now *Sports Review of the Year*, like any programme, has a certain pace to it. No item should be too long, the mix and the running order should be well-balanced, and the whole intention is to build up the tension to a nice climax at the end when the winner of the trophy is announced. So you can understand that having driven the proceedings towards a great denouement, the whole occasion can flop if the guest's speech goes on too long.

After a minute or two, Colonel Mike seemed set for a very long address indeed. I heard in my ear an instruction from the producer, Brian Venner, to the floor manager, Chris Lewis. 'Right, Chris' he said, confidently. 'Wrap him up now.' Wrap him up! Wrap him up? How, for heaven's sake?

There are several signals given to television performers by floor managers that the viewers never see, to tell them how long they've got and when to bring an interview to a close. Sometimes they are used as an alternative to the old deaf aid in the ear, and the interviewer picks them up out of the corner of his eye from the floor manager, who is standing out of vision alongside the camera. One finger means one minute left. Crossed arms means half a minute. A slow circular movement of the hand means wind it up slowly. A sudden 'cut throat' movement – across the throat with the edge of the hand – means get out now at all costs. Wrap Colonel Sir Mike up? How, for heaven's sake, when the man was blind.

That evening we reluctantly awarded to the Colonel the all-comers' record for the longest *Review of the Year* speech in the history of the programme: twelve minutes thirty-five seconds is a record that stands to this day, and we hope it will stand forever!

10

A NATIONWIDE DAY

It is Tuesday, 6 May 1980, the first programme day of another *Nationwide* week. Yesterday was a bank holiday and sport ruled, but this Tuesday is a day that presents a particular challenge: to follow up a major news story that broke last night. The hostages in the Iranian Embassy siege had been released by a cuttingly efficient operation by troops of the Special Air Service. On BBC-1, John Wayne had been left to his celluloid heroics for a real life, *Boys' Own Paper* thriller that was covered live from, of all places, Princes Gate, Kensington, in London. Even the final of the World Snooker Championship on BBC-2 was interrupted for news reports. Explosions, hooded figures shinning down ropes, shots, stretchers, ambulances, the dead, the living, police sirens; *Kojak* for real on a sunny spring evening in London. The country, indeed the whole world, was buzzing with the news.

Now it is the day after. The Tuesday papers are bulging with the story. How is one to follow it up at 6.20pm, and more than that, add to it?

The editor of the day is Andrew Clayton, working under the programme's editor proper, Hugh Williams, and the deputy editor, David Lloyd. It is his responsibility to get it right, but on a major news day like today, the support from above and below will be total.

As Andrew and his production team meet at 8.30am, his prime objective of the day, helped by his researchers, is to secure somehow an interview with some, or one, of the hostages who have been released. There is no real substitute for hearing from someone who was actually involved. The personality of the day is Police Constable Trevor Lock, the policeman who was on duty at the door of the Iranian Embassy when the terrorists struck, and who spent the whole of the five days inside. Early enquiries suggest that he is going to be difficult to get hold of. If criminal charges are to be brought against the one surviving terrorist, then it is likely that the first we will know of what happened to PC Lock is in court.

There are two other possibilities. Simeon Harris, a BBC sound recordist, had been in the embassy applying for a visa when the place was seized. His escape across a balcony at the front of the building at the height of the SAS's assault was seen by millions of television viewers all over the world. The trouble is, he is a BBC television news man, and no doubt our colleagues in television news will be anxious to sit on him for themselves to reveal his own account of what happened in the main nine o'clock news that evening. A further complication is that all the surviving hostages, Trevor Lock and Sim Harris included, have been whisked away to a secret police rendez-vous for debriefing. Early on this Tuesday morning there is no knowing when they will emerge.

By the time I arrive in the *Nationwide* office with the other presenters, who that day are John Stapleton, Bob Wellings and Sue Cook, an outline plan of action and a speculative running order have been drafted.

At the top of the list is a replay of the assault on the embassy the previous evening – a reminder of the dramatic pictures of the explosions, the attack and the shots. Then we somehow have to hear from the police in charge of the exercise of the thinking that led to the decision to send in the SAS, and the events that dictated that course of action. There is to be a police press conference later that day. John Stapleton is detailed to attend.

Next we have to establish some information about the SAS, who have so captured the public imagination, and who are the other heroes of the hour. They are anonymous and secretive, specially trained, specially armed. How was the unit created, what have they done in the past, what is their role today, and how did they go about this particular assignment? All these are questions the world is asking and to which we must try and find the answers. A military correspondent from one of the national newspapers is contacted. Yes, he has a fair idea, and he will try to improve his knowledge before he appears on the programme that evening.

Then there is the political aspect. How is the successful ending of the siege going to affect our standing with various countries in the world? In the west, the outcome is bound to be received with great pleasure. The democracies, against whom most acts of hijack and hostage-taking are directed, are inevitably delighted when law and order solves the problem, and comes out winning. Such events act as a great deterrent to other ambitious terrorists.

Finally, we must find out who the Iranians in Britain are, how many of them there are, and why they are here. Can they come and go as they please? Should action now be taken to control and monitor their entry more rigorously?

The plans for the programme are beginning to take shape. A great amount of concentrated work is now necessary to bring them to fruition. To start with a blank sheet at 8.30am, and have an hour's television on the air at 5.55pm is an intimidating challenge for the editor.

Andrew has a further decision to make. Should he devote the whole part of network *Nationwide,* from 6.20pm to 6.59pm, to the story? Will it carry at that length? Perhaps we should turn to other, lighter topics at the end. He decides we should, and plans to show a short film, a report from James Hogg in Leeds on an inner city school that has dancing lessons for both boys and girls. We also arrange to do an interview with Cliff Thorburn of Canada, who, in the middle of the drama last night, was coolly beating Alex 'Hurricane' Higgins in the final of the World Snooker Championship in Sheffield.

Almost as a matter of course, the on-the-day film crew, with Glyn Worsnip as reporter, have gone to Kensington to shoot a 'morning after the night before' film about the aftermath of the siege. 'On-the-day', because the film is shot in the morning, processed, cut, and commentary dubbed on in the afternoon, and transmitted in the evening.

It is now late morning. Everybody, particularly our young researchers, are chasing madly, telephoning constantly, trying to assemble all the pieces, to get the facts of the story as straight as they possibly can be, bearing in mind that the police so far have said very little. We have hopes that more light will be shed at the police press conference later in the afternoon. John has already established with them that PC Lock is saying nothing. He will appear at the press conference for photos, but that's all, so he's a non-starter from our point of view.

What time, then, will Sim Harris emerge from the police debriefing? The estimated time gets later and later, and anyway there is the inevitable feeling that BBC news will keep him under wraps for the big I Was There interview at

9pm. Gloomily, we admit we would probably do the same if he was our man!

Each presenter has his particular task. John is to concentrate his preparation on anything to do with the police, and for that he will attend the police press conference as decided earlier. The news outside broadcast unit will be there, and he will use that for coverage of the conference itself, and any personal interviews he can get afterwards. Bob is to apply himself to anything that may arise in the political sense. Adam Raphael, a leading political journalist, has been engaged to speculate on that issue. Bob is also thinking about and preparing for the Iranian angle. I am to prepare an interview on the history, exploits, and role of the SAS.

It is early afternoon. One of our eagle-eyed researchers has discovered the identity of a former head of the SAS. He would be terrific value, but she can't find him. She has left telephone messages by the dozen at places where he might call that afternoon.

In mid-afternoon, we discover that the incoming bank of *Nationwide* telephones have been faulty for at least an hour. Heavens only knows how many potential contributors have been trying to contact us and given up in despair.

By 4pm the script is being written by a multitude of people, each of whom devotes his or her concentration to a pertinent part. Clips of the videotape of the explosion are collected, as are still pictures (on slides) of all the participants. In the Commons Mrs Thatcher has spoken in glowing terms of the success of the mission. An American senator has said the same in Washington. We have recorded both of them, and extracts from their remarks are being selected to be fitted in at the right time.

Suddenly, several hours of telephoning bears fruit. We have the former head of the SAS on the phone. The researcher puts him on hold, gallops up to me and says: 'He's happy to do it as long as he remains in silhouette during the interview and has a conversation now with the person who is doing the interview and that's you. I'll transfer him to you.'

A strange conversation follows.

'Good afternoon.' Rich, deep voice. 'Who is that?'

'This is Frank Bough. I'm to do the interview with you – it's very, very kind of you to agree. We much appreciate it.'

He is exceedingly brusque to say the least. 'Now listen', he said, rather too arrogantly, I thought. 'If I'm to do this interview I insist on several guarantees. One – I remain in complete darkness the whole interview, otherwise I'll walk out. There are still some about who would like to find me out.'

'Agreed' – that's me.

'Two. Before the interview begins I want to be able to see on a television monitor that I am truly unrecognisable otherwise I'll walk out.'

'Agreed.'

'Three. Before the interview begins I will have a further conversation with you about the line of questioning, otherwise I'll walk out.'

'Agreed.'

'By the way', he added, a little more pleasantly, 'I'd got you down as more of a sporting type than somebody who gets involved with serious affairs like this.'

It was the same old story, but it did help to break the ice. Prime ministers, trade union leaders, Arthur Negus, heads of SAS – whoever they are they have a favourite football team and they want to tell you about it!

'Well', says I, 'there are those who reckon that there's nothing more serious in this world than sport.'

'I'm inclined to agree with you', he replied.

He hung up then, satisfied that his conditions would be met, The curious thing was that I knew who he was, indeed his father had been one of my World War II heroes. Despite all his concern about darkness and anonymity, too, under his name in *Who's Who* it says 'former head of the SAS'!

We are now within two hours of transmission. Attention switches to the bank of monitor screens at one end of the big open office. There are no partitions, no prestigious office units. Everyone, from editors to typists to messenger boy, sits together. It is important that conversations should be overheard, information shared and progress publicly measured.

On one of the monitor sets, pictures are coming in via the news outside broadcast cameras of the press conference being held at Scotland Yard. PC Lock arrives with his wife – the hero of the hour. It is slowly becoming clear that this forty-one-year-old constable, who to date has done nothing more exciting than stand as a token guard outside the door of one of London's many embassies, has performed admirably and been the prop and staff of the hostages during the five days of the siege.

We can see John Stapleton in amongst the press, ready to

make his presence felt. John is a real journalist's journalist. His preparation for a job is always meticulously done, he is scrupulously fair, and always conducts his interviews in a courteous yet properly enquiring and searching manner. No doubt he has already arranged to do a personal interview with the policeman handling the affair after the conference is over.

He has. He has got the number one man, Deputy Assistant Commissioner Dellow. John is joining *Panorama* soon; *Nationwide* will miss him.

By now, the big board on which our programme running order is detailed is beginning to take shape. Every item has a number and a name. Item One is always the programme headlines, divided between what is in part one of the programme, i.e. that seen by viewers in London and the south-east, and part two, the network part of *Nationwide* when all the regional programmes join in which starts at 6.20. Item Two today, the first south-east piece of the programme, is to be Glyn Worsnip on the day film of the aftermath of the siege. Opposite every item is written every conceivable piece of information about it: which of the presenters is introducing it, whether it is on film or videotape, which machine is running it, who the interviewees are, their titles, whether slides are needed, which researcher is responsible for the item, even down to which individual camera on the studio floor is to be used. At a glance, every detail of what is needed to make that item work is clearly visible.

Every morsel of every item is being timed, to the second; introductions, film, videotape, length of interviews. Everything has to fit exactly. There are several precise times that have to be met during the programme, particularly at 6.20 as I have explained. It is decided that there is no room for Cliff Thorburn. He is stood down, politely; not needed.

With half-an-hour to go at about 5.30pm, what have we got? How far have we fulfilled our intentions of the morning? We have got Glyn Worsnip's colour piece on the siege aftermath. We have a reconstruction of the siege climax, blow by blow. We have the police follow-up well covered, both with the press conference and John's interviews. My SAS item has a promising look about it. After all, we have got our man in silhouette who once ran the organisation.

Hugh Williams wants to know how I plan to tackle the interview. He feels that since the man is going to be discreet, not to say cagey, I should ask simple, direct questions which will at least force him to be as informative as possible. I explain my approach. How was the attack on the embassy planned? What information about the occupants, their disposition and weapons did the SAS have? Did each man have a particular role? What arms did they carry? Is it true that they are allowed to choose their own? What about the explosives? When they went off, how did the grenades not kill everybody inside? When the SAS got inside, in the split seconds they had to decide, how did they know who was friend and who was foe? Hugh threw in a couple of questions I hadn't though of, but basically we were both thinking along the same lines.

Andrew Clayton was getting more and more agitated, his way of getting himself sharpened up. He always does, but today is a special day. As the editor of the day, it is all his responsibility. He's anxious to win every second of the way.

The political aspect of the affair, with Adam Raphael and the Iranian community in London, is well covered. Vahe Petrossian, an expert on Iranian matters, is being interviewed by Bob. What we haven't got, what nobody has got, is a hostage, to tell us what it was like in there. Lock is under wraps, Harris is clearly being hidden away by news department – and indeed, later that evening does appear on the 9pm news to give a marvellously descriptive account of what happened to him and the others when the SAS broke into the embassy.

Scripts are being checked and typed, and here again there is a system. They are written, checked, typed, checked, autocued, checked, and then ticked off as done on the big board. Every possibility of error is eliminated.

Most days at 5.30, the programme is ready and scripts are completed. I spend the next ten minutes, always, putting the scripts in order, one for each item, and reading through them out loud. I familiarise myself with the contents, and with the sound of the words and sentences, even now questioning a fact or rewriting a phrase to my own satisfaction.

At twenty to six, fifteen minutes before the programme begins, I go down to the studio. The other presenters are normally there already. That's their habit. As usual Bob is sinking deeper into himself, into a kind of professional incommunicado state. I try not to be too hearty, as is *my* wont, because it infuriates him as I have told you.

My SAS man has not yet arrived. This is a slight worry, compounded by the fact that if he arrives after the programme starts I may not be able to reassure him as to his anonymity, or discuss the questioning with him. Time for make-up – more often than not, the girl will come out of her cubical on to the studio floor to dull the shine on my brow, because I haven't time to go to her. Deaf aid in. Mike clipped to tie. Radio receiver and transmitter, each slid into a pouch attached to the back of my belt. Talkback checked. Nigel, the director, switches in to our ears, checking in turn that each one of us can hear him. As I have explained, it is switched talkback, so that only when we are given specific instructions, or counted down into videotape or film, will we hear anything from the gallery. We have a quick headlines rehearsal, the only rehearsal we ever get. One minute to transmission. Titles are running – we're on the air.

At the end of the title music, Nigel in the ear: *'Opt out, opt out – cue Bob.'* The plugs have been pulled out, thirteen regions leave us, and Bob gives the London and the south-east headlines. Thirteen regional presenters are doing the same, speaking to their own audiences from Plymouth to Newcastle, Cardiff, Belfast and Glasgow. Each speaks for precisely seventeen seconds. Nigel again, *'Opt in, opt in – cue Frank'*. The plugs are back in, to enable me to speak to the whole country. 'And at 6.20 the storming of Princes Gate. In the aftermath of the siege at the Iranian Embassy we report in detail on how the crack commandos freed the hostages. We talk to the policeman who led the operation and ask: could they have done it earlier? On a lighter note we visit a school in Leeds where dancing is compulsory and competes with the three Rs and games for the pupils' loyalty. That's after your own programmes, nationwide.' Twenty-one seconds precisely. A sting (a phrase) of music while Nigel says *'Opt out, opt out'*. Plugs away, and for twenty-five minutes we all have our regional programmes.

Once *Nationwide* has started, if each member of the team has done his or her job properly, then all should proceed according to the plans, with each piece of the jigsaw plopping into place at its appointed time. Link, film, slide, presenter in the right place, in front of the right part of the set; videotape runs, camera cuts, words, pictures. As ever, the big uncertainties are the interviews. My ex-head of the SAS, I discover, has arrived and is in the Green Room, the small anteroom adjacent to the studio, where guests are held just before they appear.

In the studio, we are working out way towards 6.20, when we are joined by the rest of the country and embark on our big feature on the siege. In the end Bob has the job of getting to it on time, with an interview, the last item of our south-east regional section. The Turner collection of paintings, it has been announced that day, are to be housed under one roof for the first time. '*Two minutes to the opt*' comes from the gallery. Bob is measuring his way through the interview with an art expert. '*One minute to the opt.*' Bob has to leave fifteen seconds at the end of his piece, in which Sue Cook will do the south-east weather forecast. '*Twenty seconds to the opt.*' Bob has made it neatly: 'Thank you very much.' Sue embarks on the weather. '*10-9-8-7-6-5-4-3-2-1 – opt in, opt in.*'

In thirteen regional centres the same thing is happening; as the second hand on the gallery clock hits 6.20, the plugs go in and we're all together again.

'*Cue Frank.*'

'Welcome, now that we're together nationwide. Tonight we'll be bringing you in detail last night's dramatic events at the London embassy siege. At the moment, the hostages are still going through a debriefing session with the police, so there's still no peace for them today. But meanwhile we'll be looking at the methods the police used leading up to yesterday's storming of the embassy by the elite Special Air Service, and we'll be piecing together the scanty information about the SAS, explaining the role they played yesterday and what they've done in the past.'

At the appropriate moment, while we are transmitting the videotape recording of John's police press conference, the distinguished former head of the SAS is brought on to the set. Much to my astonishment he is now affability personified. Gone is the tense, staccato approach he adopted on the telephone – the demands, the conditions. We've fulfilled them anyway, but all he wants to talk about in the few seconds we have before the interview is the series of FA Cup replays he's been watching between Arsenal and Liverpool! Then we're on, he shrouded in darkness, though I can see him quite clearly. Only the electronic camera eye, denied its essential light on the subject, assures his anonymity to the viewer, as I fire away with my direct questions. He responds well and gives me a very good interview without betraying any of the secrets of the SAS.

The programme runs its length. It is all good, workmanlike

journalism, backed by super-efficient television presentation from all the areas of the programme. As Bob rounds off the siege story on the subject of Iranians in Britain, it is Sue Cook who finds herself with a fairly common *Nationwide* presenter's dilemma: to turn the subject matter from that of life and death to something light and frothy. She must adjust the tone from death at the Iranian Embassy to the boys and girls at a Leeds City School, where they are encouraged to dance their way to a better and more civilised adulthood. She does it neatly, and as the film rolls through, all that remains is to close the programme and get off the air with dignity.

In the gallery, the producer's assistant does her arithmetic. I have ten seconds in which to say goodnight, yet also to explain that because of the death of President Tito of Yugoslavia, Mrs Margaret Thatcher will not, as planned, be in the studio with us tomorrow night, but at a later, rearranged date.

'Ten seconds left on film.'

'Stand by Frank – cue Frank.'

I devise a neat form of words to length – *'10-9-8-7-6-5-4-3-2-1 – we're off the air.'*

Let me allow Stuart Wilkinson again to provide the last word. '*Nationwide* is now something of a nightly institution, the place where the audience expects to see the day's events reported and their implications discussed and where, within the same hour, they will undoubtedly find much to amuse and entertain.'

So, watch *Panorama*, and it will not surprise you to encounter the prime minister or the leader of the opposition. Watch *Tonight* (as it was then) and you may well find an engaging personality from the West End theatre or Hollywood; watch *Newsday* and it will occur to you as totally unsurprising to find there the important trade union leader or the chairman of a nationalised industry. Try *Nationwide* and you may well discover the armless darts player, a beer-drinking snail, a mother giving birth and a man playing *Land of Hope and Glory* on a watering can. Or you may find the prime minister, the leader of the opposition, the trade unionist or the showbiz personality. The *Nationwide* addict has seen them all.

11

END-TITLES

I once heard a radio programme in which the proposition was made that we should all, at the age of forty, stop doing what we are doing and do something else. It was suggested that a huge majority of people go through life reasonably content, or perhaps as miserable as sin, but unaware that somewhere is another job, another life, for which we are far more suited; and, furthermore, that most of us have a gift for doing something really well, but that we are unlikely to find out what it is.

A stimulating theory. Sadly, having made our pitch at life, by the age of forty we are, generally speaking, stuck with it. We have a mortgage to pay, a family to feed, and economic necessity dictates that we stick in the rut we have decided upon. It does just that, too, however little we may like the taste of our lives.

Having read what you have just read, how can I persuade you that I am restless to know what I should do next. I have achieved neither financial independence, since the next bill to be paid depends on the next programme fee; nor have I achieved total satisfaction, since I have had to spend too much time neglecting the one thing that has given me most pleasure, and which is more important than anything I've yet found, which is the family. I have served my television apprenticeship in the best days of the medium in which I work. Nothing in television can be more exciting than the sixties and seventies have been. The pioneering days in anything are always the best. Progress is made in a succession of exciting leaps and bounds. Nowadays, improvement is measured, like the mile, in fractions of a second.

In the BBC, progress is retarded by economic restrictions. It is becoming increasingly difficult, if not impossible, to maintain the standards that the Corporation has set, let alone seek new heights of excellence, which is what we should be doing.

End-Titles

No wonder customers are critical. Yet what right have we to complain – and I say we, because I am a customer as well as a salesman – when we pay nine pence a day for two television channels, four radio channels, and all the local radio we can digest? Nine pence a day. Less than *The Sun* newspaper. About a fifth of the price of a pint of beer.

Perhaps the man on the radio was right. Perhaps there is another challenge, something I can do better. This year, 1980, I'm forty-seven. I embark on my thirteenth year with *Grandstand*, my ninth with *Nationwide*. Tell me: is it too late? What should we all do next?